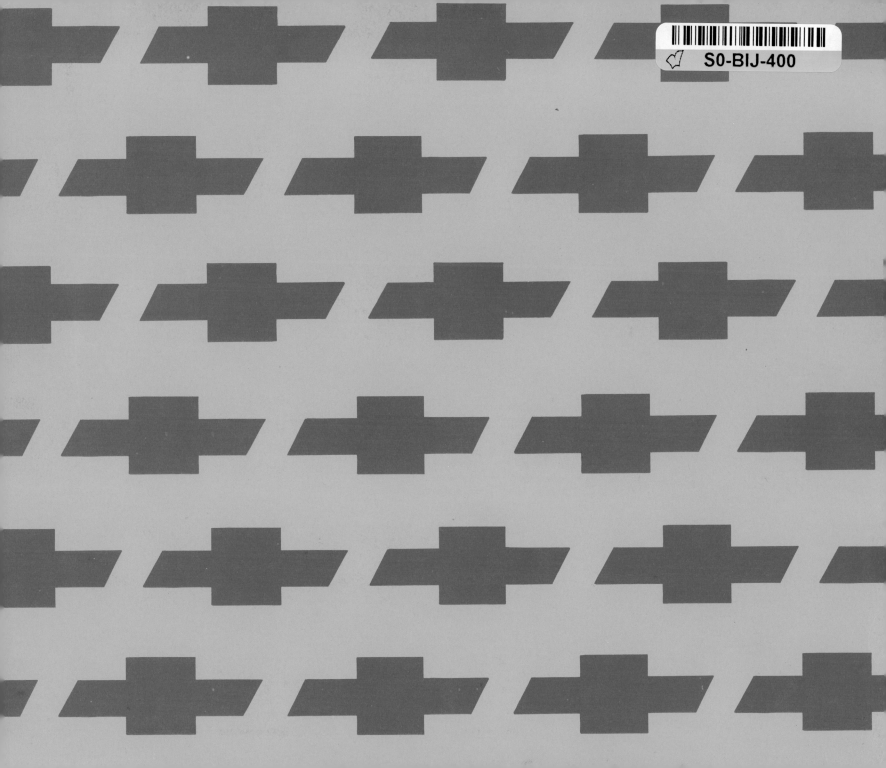

THE HOT ONE
Chevrolet : 1955-1957

THE HOT ONE
Chevrolet: 1955-1957

By Pat Chappell

*To Dave,
who belongs to the
fraternity of
automotive enthusiasts.
Best wishes,
Pat Chappell*

1955
1957

DRAGONWYCK PUBLISHING LTD.
BOX 385, CONTOOCOOK, NEW HAMPSHIRE 03229

Design by Taylor-Constantine, Grandview-on-Hudson, New York
Typography by Eagle Spring Press, Nyack, New York
Printing by Michael Graphics, New Brunswick, New Jersey
Binding by N.H. Bindery, Inc., Concord, New Hampshire

THIRD EDITION THIRD PRINTING • 1984

Library of Congress Cataloging in Publication Data

Chappell, Pat
  The hot one.

  Includes index.
  1. Chevrolet automobile. I. Title.
TL 215.C5C45   629.22'22   77-21298
ISBN 0-9606148-0-X

Dedicated To:

THE MEN WHO DESIGNED, ENGINEERED,
 BUILT AND DROVE THEM,
AND ALL WHO ENJOY THEM TODAY:

 1955-1957 CHEVROLETS

Contents

Foreword

Twenty years ago an era ended. Many who admire the cars of the past think of it as a golden age for Chevrolet, a happy time with some of their best memories made driving 1955-57 Chevys. Though the appreciation never fully diminished, it has been rekindled today with perhaps even greater enthusiasm by restorers and collectors of these same, outstanding automobiles.

Two key men in the development of "The Hot One" were Edward N. Cole—who died when his private plane crashed on May 2nd, 1977—and the late Harley J. Earl. They were responsible for the all-new image of Chevrolet in 1955, that launched it on these three significant years.

Today, an examination of those cars is appropriate: many involved in their design are still active and reachable, yet the writer can now be fully objective. But even the objective author cannot fail to be impressed by the premise of "team effort," not only at GM today, but throughout the story of the 1955-57 Chevy.

My list of acknowledgements is long, and very important to me. Designers Clare M. MacKichan, chief of the Chevrolet studio during the 1955-57 program, Carl H. Renner, Bob Cadaret, Bob Veryzer and Chuck A. Stebbins were all instrumental in grounding the test in accuracy. Vince W. Piggins, presently manager of Chevrolet Product Promotion, recalled the Division's involvement in racing during the mid-Fifties. At GM Public Relations, Joseph H. Karshner, Jim Williams, Gloria Jezewski and H.J. Cordes were all invaluable in locating sources and photographs. Research material was graciously provided by Jim Bradley of the National Automotive History Collection, Detroit Public Library, and Mary Cattie of the Free Library of Philadelphia; Henry Austin Clark, Jr., and Edward H. Still each provided material from their private collections. The manuscript was subjected to the critical eyes of Messrs. MacKichan, Piggins, Renner and Stebbins of General Motors, along with Nelson E. Aregood, Dick Baty, Dick Fusco, Wayne E. Oakley and Joe Umphenour of the National Nomad Club.

Artistic endeavors played an important part in the presentation of this material, thanks to Myron Scott's creative photography for General Motors 20 years ago. Much of it enhances the following pages. Russ von Sauers illustrated the dust jacket, Jean and Rich Taylor were responsible for the overall design. The advertising artwork for Chevrolet, circa 1955-57, was gathered for us by Mike Rosenberg of Campbell-Ewald, the Chevy ad agency lo these many years. William S. Jackson was the printer. And, lest we forget, Chevrolet Division of General Motors produced the car which made all this possible.

Four men gave me the added incentive to make this book a reality--in quite different ways. Tom Warth, president of Motorbooks International, listened to my scheme and encouraged me to follow up. Carl Renner opened his home, his heart, his portfolio--and a few doors as well. Richard M. Langworth, as editor, was the matchless embodiment of editors everywhere, curmudgeonly and critical, merciless and good. Finally, my husband Dick, one of the many millions to whom this book is dedicated, who drove one then and still does today, has shared my ambition to see this story told.

I have contemplated writing only one book. This one seemed an ideal choice. I hope you enjoy it.

Pat Chappell
Wilmington, Delaware
May, 1977

These two Chevrolets were milestones for General Motors: 25 millionth production car (1940), 50 millionth (1955).

CHAPTER ONE

Almost Everybody Had One Once

Glistening as it rolled off the assembly line, a golden Chevrolet celebrated General Motors' 50 millionth production car. The date was November 23rd, 1954; the place, Flint, Michigan; the car, a 1955 Bel Air sport coupe. It was all very fitting.

The 1955 Chevrolet represented a watershed in the long and success-studded history of General Motors. It was brand new, in styling, engineering and sales image, bearing Chevrolet's first successful V-8 engine, aimed at the constituency which for the past 20 years had been mainly Ford's. Yet it was intended to do that which Chevrolet had always done: account for about 60 percent of the corporation's automobiles.

A month before, the 1955 Chevy line made its public debut in showrooms throughout the country. Public acceptance had been high, reassuring GM that the Chevrolet Division would retain its number one position in the industry, held since 1936. Almost fifteen years before, on January 11th, 1940, a silver Chevrolet had marked GM's 25-millionth car; now, the city of Flint celebrated its doubling

of that number. "Chevrolet Leads the Way," was the slogan of the 100,000-plus guest party, with open house festivities at the Flint plants, a parade featuring five bands, and thousands of sub-events simultaneously held throughout the country. "Open House to America" encompassed luncheons in 22 cities in which Chevrolet had 30 manufacturing or assembly plants, and on closed circuit television 82,000 Chevy employees heard GM president Harlow H. Curtice thank them for their share in the production feat.

The golden Chevy--more precisely the 1955 Chevrolet--touched off a grand era for this GM Division. For the next three years, it would build what are probably the three most memorable lines of cars in its long history, and some of the most famous in the even longer history of General Motors Corporation.

General Motors. There is hardly anyone alive who hasn't felt its impact, the impact of a company that consistently, in bad times and good, made the right decisions, built the right cars at the right time. GM had meager be-

Above, GM president Harlow Curtice appears at a preview of the historic 1955 Golden Chevrolet, GM's 50,000,000th automobile.

Above right, a silver 1940 sport sedan perched on float in "Open House to America" parade in Flint, Michigan, late 1954.

Below right, golden Bel Air sport coupe bedecked with flowers and a model, celebrating the memorable production milestone.

ginnings, and fumbled at times--Chevrolet was once considered for oblivion as a bad risk at a time when Ford dominated the industry--but for the most part GM has been an incredible success. It has, in many respects, reflected the economic prosperity of the country at large. To paraphrase that oft-misquoted statement of Charles Wilson's,* "What's Good for GM"... what was good for Chevrolet was also good for General Motors.

Any company as large and successful as GM makes a very inviting target. It has been the subject of investigation, anti-trust litigation and bombast by opponents both within and without government; accused of monopolistic tendencies, blasted by authors profound and fatuous, knowledgeable and ignorant. No one climbs to the top of a mountain without someone waiting below to knock him off, although as far as GM is concerned that possibility is remote. The company arrived where it is today on the basis of sound management, imagination and common sense. In an industry where a firm can survive, usually, by making seven out of ten right decisions, General Motors has probably been right nine times out of ten, or better. The success of the corporation is pertinent to the 1955-57 Chevrolet story, because those cars owed their intrinsic excellence to managerial policies, a design and engineering department, a sales and dealer network, developed years before.

General Motors' secret of success was its basic organizational philosophy, defined by Alfred P. Sloan, Jr. as "coordinated decentralization." Said Sloan, "decision-making is delegated to lower levels of management, but all decisions are both patterned by corporate policies and continuously checked and approved, preshaped and reshaped by a few top executives at headquarters...from decentralization

* Charles E. Wilson, while Secretary of Defense under Eisenhower, stated, "What's good for our country was good for General Motors, and vice-versa." The vice-versa is often quoted by the media, though it was never actually stated in the reverse order.

we get initiative, responsibility, development of personnel, decisions close to the facts, flexibility--in short, all the qualities necessary for an organization to adapt to new conditions. From coordination we get efficiencies and economies. It must be apparent that coordinated decentralization is not an easy concept to apply. There is no hard and fast rule for sorting out the various responsibilities and the best way to assign them. The balance which is struck between corporate and divisional responsibility varies according to what is being decided, the circumstances of the time, past experience, and the temperaments and skills of the executives involved."

Like much in GM's history, "Coordinated decentralization" developed and expanded through trial and error, and not without growing pains. But it usually worked. When it didn't, it was partially modified to suit the situation.

GM headquarters on West Grand Boulevard, Detroit, Michigan

Alfred P. Sloan, Jr., Pres. 1923-37.

William S. Knudsen, Pres. 1937-40.

Charles Wilson, GM President 1941-53.

Chevy Division Chief Thomas Keating

"Experience has convinced me," Sloan continued, "that for those who are responsible for a business, two important factors are motivation and opportunity. The former is supplied in good part by incentive compensation, the latter by decentralization. But the matter does not end there. It has been [my thesis] that good management rests on a reconciliation of centralization and decentralization or 'decentralization with coordinated control.'"

Alfred Sloan's painstakingly detailed system combined with an alert competitiveness among the divisions to promote the growth and efficiency of GM as a whole. Divisional competition, *Fortune* said, "is designed to combine with cooperation at headquarters to provide more sales and headier ideas. GM lives on newness, and the five auto chiefs hold their jobs by helping to create it."

In 1962, General Motors was the largest of private industrial enterprises, with over a million stockholders, 600,000 employees, $9.2 billion in assets, $14.6 billion in sales, and $1.46 billion in profits--a distinction, Sloan said, that makes it a political target. But Sloan had a telling rationale for the sheer size of his company: "Size," he said, "is the outcome of competitive performance; when it comes to making things like automobiles and locomotives in large numbers...a large size is fitting. It should not be forgotten that the dollar value of these products is relatively high; even a 'small' automobile producer may rank among the first hundred largest industrial corporations...Growth, or striving for it, is, I believe, essential to the good health of an enterprise. Deliberately to stop growing is to suffocate."

Sloan, and GM, put "no ceiling on progress." In 1956, a *Fortune* writer asked then-president Harlow H. Curtice, "You now have 50 percent of the industry's business. Would you like to try for 55 or 60 percent?" Curtice replied, "We have no control over the public's approval...We know no other way than to do our best--our utmost. How can you deliberately restrain your performance and remain healthy and progressive? How can you put an artificial limit on size and still preserve the free enterprise system?" That was and is General Motors' dilemma. Many envy it.

It was that "superb shopman" William Knudsen, a giant in GM history, who first supplied the impetus to Chevrolet in its drive to the top of the industry. Knudsen established the "one-for-one" criteria--building one Chevrolet for every Ford. Under Knudsen the Chevy dealer corps grew in *Fortune's* words, "into a distributive organization that remains the envy and despair of every other carmaker. And he gave Chevrolet its air of relative independence among GM divisions, if only by his penchant for settling any argument with the flat statement, 'Ve go the Chevrolet vay.'" This was the beginning of Chevy's serious challenge to Ford. It surpassed Ford in the late Twenties, as Dearborn paused to replace Model T with Model A, and with one or two exceptions it has been ahead of Ford ever since.

Also crucial in the Chevy success story was Thomas H. Keating, division manager from 1949 to mid-1956, when the race between Ford and Chevrolet was at its hottest. Keating, a Chevrolet man since 1916, began as a distributor and worked his way up through the sales department. He ran the division in typical GM fashion, delegating responsibility to senior managers for sales, engineering, manufacturing and finance, meeting with them usually once a month, using assistants to coordinate their efforts. He also oversaw 31 plants and 7500 dealers. Keating was responsible for evolving the Bel Air two-door hardtop of 1950 into a whole series of Bel Air models by 1953, a fancy dressed up line which made sales soar. He was hampered by the Korean War shortages in bringing out an entirely new line of Chevrolets, but he finally did so in 1953, a slight disadvantage as he was a year behind Ford. But Chevy outsold Ford anyway, and for 1955 geared up for the all-new cars that were to write industry legend. Keating respected the "youth market," he and Curtice realized that the six-cylinder engine was inappropriate in that respect, so Keating brought engineer Ed Cole over from Cadillac to develop a lightweight, performance V-8 for Chevrolet. The '55 owed a lot to Thomas H. Keating.

Harlow H. Curtice, GM president during the 1955-57 period, was the man at the top who inspired the corporation as a whole, and a key figure in the 1955-57 Chevrolet. Born in 1893, the son of a wholesale produce man, he worked his way through the Ferris Institute in Big Rapids, Michigan. He then joined AC Spark Plug as a bookkeeper and at age 21 became controller of this GM subsidiary. A brief interlude with the Army during World War I was followed by progression to AC assistant general manager, vice-president and--at age 35--president. Five years later, in 1933, GM vice-president Knudsen called on Curtice to save a faltering Buick Division, whose production had dropped from 240,000 to less than 45,000 cars a year.

Curtice ran Buick with a vengeance. He reduced the price of the cars, called in Harley Earl to come up with a new, lighter, less expensive model named the Special. He ousted inefficient personnel, released Buick sales from central distribution office control, and reestablished "coordinated decentralization." Then he took to the road in an exhaustive dealer pep talk and revival campaign. Finally, he turned the image of Buick from a staid car for stuffy types into a youthful bombshell, "Dressed for a Party--Powered for a Thrill."

It paid off handsomely. Buick sales increased 44 percent within Curtice's first year. In four years, sales had

Motorama show cars often featured styling techniques that gauged public reaction. Such a model was Cadillac's two-place El Camino...

And another was the convertible, La Espada. Future production Cadillacs soon adopted similar fins, bumper bullets, minor trim.

quadrupled to over 200,000, and Buick had shot past Dodge, Pontiac and Oldsmobile into fourth place in the industry. It was GM's second biggest money maker. By 1941, Buick was up to 300,000 cars and over eight percent of the market. After the war, in 1948, Curtice was made executive vice-president for staff operations, and in 1953, when president Charles E. Wilson was called to Washington, Harlow Curtice became president of General Motors.

Curtice was responsible for the twelve-month retooling program for the 1954 Buick and Oldsmobile, which saw them on the showroom floors "all new" in January, 1954. Their wrapped windshields and dropped beltlines not only predicted styling trends to come at Chevrolet and Pontiac, but enabled GM to garner more than 50 percent of the market for the first time. A popular joke at the time went, "Whenever the company's 51 percent share is mentioned, someone is sure to say, 'You know what the boss says-- that means we're losing almost five out of every ten deals.' " Harlow's motto, he said, was "run like Hell in order to stand still." Because of his forcefulness and lack of complacency, GM continued to remain number one, though chased constantly in this period by Ford Motor Company. Not only did he possess extraordinary financial talent, but he could understand and predict styling trends; coupled with Harley Earl's styling team, Harlow Curtice emerged as central to a distinguished period in GM history.

Curtice also understood the concepts of salable engineering developments and coordinated production. Though schedules at GM were usually set many months in advance, changes were made as often as every ten days. When the 1956 cars were announced, for example, the production overlap was only 0.7 percent, or one and one-half cars per dealer. Curtice got the credit for that, and he richly deserved it.

Perhaps the most influencing factor in automobile sales is styling, and one can hardly discuss GM styling without

Harley J. Earl headed GM Styling Section, 1927-1958.

mentioning the legendary Harley Earl. Famous for such statements as "a greyhound is more graceful than a bulldog," Earl once described his primary career mission "to lengthen and lower the American automobile, at times in reality and always at least in appearance." Founder of GM's Art and Colour Section, Earl developed it over the years to a highly complex organization, reflecting the overriding policy of controlled decentralization, and competition among the divisions.

Earl's father was a carriage manufacturer in Los Angeles, and even as an engineering student at Stanford, young Harley enjoyed his drawing courses. The automobile, of course, was his major subject. His father produced broughams and landaus for the California carriage trade, and Earl soon joined in the family business. "The first automobile body that I undertook was built behind my father's back, " he said in one reminiscence. "I think I am justified in saying that my career started in a big way. My first order for a special auto body was from Fatty Arbuckle." Earl continued to promote and receive orders from the *ton* of Hollywood society, and his fame grew accordingly.

Cadillac head Lawrence P. Fisher, and GM president Sloan, brought Earl to Detroit at the age of 32. His first project was the design of a small Cadillac, the LaSalle, for 1927. It was a revelation--sleek, glamorous, entirely new; a brilliant design that is still held exemplary by students of the art. "I have a great affection for the old crock," Earl said later, "but I must admit it is slab-sided, top-heavy and stiff shouldered." Earl rarely looked back.

Of the Art and Colour Section, Earl said in 1954: "We work informally and, of course, secretly. Since our job is to generate and present design ideas, we have methods of keeping new ideas popping and stirring...For my part, I often act merely as a prompter. If a particular group appears to be bogging down over a new fender or grille or interior trim, I sometimes wander into their quarters, make some irrelevant or even zany observation, and then leave. It is surprising what effect a bit of peculiar behavior will have. First-class minds will seize on anything out of the ordinary and race off looking for explanations or hidden meanings. That's all I want them to do--start exercising their imaginations. The ideas will soon pop up...We introduce a freshman squad every year, mostly from two design schools on the East and West coasts...my own little hatchery for future plans is a hidden room with no telephone, the windows blacked out and a misleading name on the door...we can't afford big mistakes and we don't even like little ones...you car buyers today are willing to accept more rapid forward jumps in style than you were twenty years ago."

Earl, it may be said, never stopped styling, if not on the drawing board then in his mind. On a street in Italy, he once noticed a small four-door custom car, without a post between the doors. The idea fermented in his mind, later to appear at the 1953 Motorama on the Cadillac Orleans show car. Many know of the famous Cadillac tailfins, which appeared in 1948; they grew from the P-38 Lockheed Lightning fighter plane Earl and his staff had seen during the war. Similarly, Earl's jet-propelled Firebird of 1954, another Motorama show car, was inspired by a picture of the new Douglas Skyray jet. Of the proportions he had developed by 1954, Earl said, "There was a time when automobiles tilted down in front, as if they intended to dig for woodchucks. Subsequently they went tail-heavy and appeared to be sitting up and begging. Now I think we have them in exactly the right attitude of level alertness, like an airplane at take-off."

The immediate postwar years were exciting ones for Harley Earl and his Art and Colour Section, for they witnessed two very important GM developments: the advent of the Motoramas and the development of the GM Technical Center in Warren, Michigan. Although the Tech Center was not formally dedicated until May of 1956, its formation began with Alfred P. Sloan, Jr. in 1944. The Motoramas were an outgrowth of Sloan's annual New York industrialist luncheons and GM shows, such as 1949's "Transportation Unlimited." The Korean War curtailed show activity, but the Motorama appeared in 1953, continued through 1956. Another was held in 1959, and the final event in 1961. Motoramas were of critical importance during the Fifties, stellar performance opportunities for the

Advanced Styling Section. They were at the same time enormous undertakings--professional shows, accompanied by professional promotion. Earl liked to think of the Motorama as a preview, where frank opinions could be expressed and recorded by GM executives and public. Another angle was that of promotion: "I saw it a few years ago at the Motorama, an experimental dream car then; but now I can actually buy it!"

Public opinion of styling was never more encouraged than at the Motoramas. GM customer relations people distributed and sorted millions of questionnaires, compiling attitudes toward production styling as well as future trends. The people came in droves--admission was always free--and their comments were spontaneous. As *Fortune* noted, "GM stylists purposely shoot their arrows in various directions to see which strike the public fancy."

"Transportation Unlimited," the 1949 show, played to audiences in New York and Boston, with attendance at nearly 600,000. The 1950 show, limited to New York, drew 320,000. The first show to bear the Motorama name was 1953's, costing GM $4.1 million and featuring several notable cars: the fiberglass Chevrolet Corvette, the sporting Cadillac LeMans, the Oldsmobile Starfire with its panoramic windshield; Buick's low, lithe Wildcat; Pontiac's Landau, with pink leather interior and black broadtail carpet. This hype promoted increased sales, to a record $9 billion, and industry-wide production to five and one-half million cars. "Our hat is knocked off every time we get in or out of any car," sniffed *The New Yorker*, but to most observers it really didn't seem so important. The 1953 show moved from New York to Miami, Houston, Los Angeles, San Francisco and Kansas City before closing with total attendance of over 1.4 million.

The 1954 Motorama was even more important to the 1955-57 Chevrolet story, for it marked the appearance of the Corvette Nomad, whose basic design went into produc-

Ed Cole and Tom Keating view Corvette at the 1953 Motorama.

With Kaiser-Darrin, Corvette was first postwar U.S. sports car.

Wrapped windshield, beltline dip in 1954 Buick (right) were innovations predating Chevrolet by one year.

"Corvair" was first coined as a GM name for this 1954 Motorama fastback, another styling prototype.

tion in 1955. The "Waldorf Nomad" was accompanied by three other interesting cars, the production Corvette and two show cars, a Corvette hardtop (a factory hardtop didn't appear until 1956), and a "Corvair" fastback coupe which never went into production in this form. The public also oohed and aahed at the new Buick, Olds and Cadillac. "Lower and longer" was still the Earl theme song, and the horsepower race was just beginning. The 1954 Cadillac borrowed features from the 1953 LeMans show car, and the striking new Oldsmobile Starfire convertible donned the name and many features of its 1953 show car predecessor. Styling ideas purely experimental or limited-production in 1953 were put into production on Oldsmobile, Buick and Cadillac in 1954: wrapped windshields, cutdown doors via beltline dips, an overall lower and longer look. The 1954 Motorama moved to Miami, Los Angeles, San Francisco and Chicago, total attendance was close to two million. Overall, GM had retooled for 25 new production models and 11 experimental cars and was coming off a 3.5 million car year with 50 percent of the car market.

The new Technical Center in Warren, "setting for a passion play of the Industrial World" as one commentator described it, was by 1954 moving toward completion. GM invested $125 million in it, and with good reason. "The inadequacy of our previous facilities was obvious even before the end of World War II," Sloan wrote later. "Our different staff operations were then scattered all over the Detroit area...I was especially struck by the unhappy situation of the Styling Staff, whose fabricating shops were located in an old Fisher Body building several miles from staff headquarters. This building was adjacent to some heavy engineering work we were doing, especially on diesel engines, and Mr. Earl's men were oppressed by the noise. In any case, they did not have enough room."

In March 1944, Sloan wrote to Charles Kettering, then head of GM Research, with the idea of a new staff center,

Corvair with star of "The Dinah Shore Chevy Show," 1954.

and "Boss Ket" responded enthusiastically. Sloan himself came up with the name. The GM Technical Center would comprise "expanded research, engineering, design and product activity areas." The land purchase, in Warren Township northeast of Detroit, was complete by mid-December 1944.

Harley Earl had desired the Tech Center's architecture to exude distinction and high aesthetic principles, while others felt it should be practical and functional. A visit to the new Ethyl Corporation Laboratories convinced Sloan to use the aesthetic approach. It was a good decision. Today, over twenty years since its opening, the GM Tech Center is still beautifully timeless.

Earl selected Eliel and Eero Saarinen as architects, and their preliminary plans were in hand by July, 1945. Postwar production absorbed the attentions of the company until 1949, but construction really got under way from

Described as "nothing less than the industrial Versailles," GM's Tech Center at Warren, Michigan, had been planned in 1944.

then on. The 900 acre site included a 22 acre artificial lake, surrounded by clusters of buildings colorfully decorated with glazed end walls of colored brick. To the north were the Research Laboratories, to the east Manufacturing and Engineering Staff, to the south Styling Staff (including a domed auditorium). This campus-like atmosphere was enhanced with gardens, islands of trees, highly manicured lawns separating the buildings. The technology involved was stupendous for 1956: high-velocity air conditioning, specially glazed brick, porcelain-enamel steel panels kept rigid by paper honeycomb fillers, a watertight gasketing sytem of neoprene for holding windows and porcelain panels in their frames.

Sloan was pleased with the Tech Center's appearance, but didn't fail to emphasize its primary role: "To get work done...perhaps its real greatness resides in the fact that it is wonderfully functional as well as elegant." Its "real greatness" was its capacity to house 4000 employees--1300 in research, 1200 in styling, 700 in engineering, 400 in process development--in 1956. There are many more today.

The aforementioned Ed Cole deserves early comment in the story of the 1955-57 Chevrolet. He was, undoubtedly, its father--the one person most responsible for achieving its performance image. Edward N. Cole, who died in a tragic crash of his private plane in 1977, was one of the wizards of the Twentieth Century. He had continued, even after his association with General Motors, to leave an indelible mark.

Many stories surround Cole's early years. There's the one about him hopping behind the wheel of his family's 1908 Buick, promptly smashing it into a tree; of his first car, a four-cylinder Saxon, which he converted into a hot rod and laid patches of rubber on the back roads of Marne, Michigan; of his many Model Ts, then his 1929 Chevrolet equipped with rocker arms from a 16-cylinder engine,

three carburetors breathing through a four-inch furnace flue. Ed Cole was always a kid about cars, always fascinated, absorbed with making them perform better than they had before.

He was born in Marne in 1909, a farm boy who rose early and got his work done fast. His interests tended toward the mechanical at an early age: there was a snowplow that he hooked to a horse to clear driveways in the winter, demonstrations with plows and Ford tractors to farmers in the summer. He tinkered with radios, and rebuilt cars.

Cole entered Grand Rapids Junior College with a law degree in mind, but he soon decided instead to enter the General Motors Institute. He took part in a work-study program affiliated with Cadillac, and in 1933 he was hired by that division as a full-time engineer. As war approached, he designed Army light tanks and combat vehicles, and a new rear engine for the M-3 light tank--the latter with a 90 day lead time. Following the war, Cole was asked to apply himself to an experimental rear-engined Cadillac-- quite an unusual design, with the engine in the back seat and dual rear tires. During this time he worked with Cadillac chief John Gordon, and in due course came his greatest achievement to date--the new Cadillac V-8.

This short-stroke engine, with high compression and light weight, appeared on the 1949 Cadillacs and became the basis for all high compression engines to follow. Cole, always economy-minded and weight-conscious, insured that it was 220 pounds lighter than the L-head V-8 it replaced, seven percent more powerful, and far more economical.

The rear engine concept continued to absorb much of Cole's energies. He came up with an air-cooled unit for a tank that was used during the Korean War, and eventually developed what became the pancake six of the rear-engine, air-cooled Corvair.

During the Korean interlude, Cole took over as works manager at the Cadillac Cleveland plant, where he served for 30 months. But Chevrolet was soon to enter his life in a big way--Chevrolet, it seemed, needed a man like him.

Chevrolet since the Twenties had an established reputation for dependability and durability, but it was still powered by the 1929 six-cylinder engine, albeit somewhat updated. The postwar sales boom was over by the early Fifties: Chevrolet sales dropped from 1.5 million in 1950 to just 878,000 in 1952, though partly due to Korean War cutbacks. Nevertheless, thought Charles Wilson and Thomas Keating, Chevrolet obviously needed a healthy transfusion of new blood. The logical choice was Cole.

Cole preferred the position of chief engineer to that of manufacturing manager which went to Ed Kelley. "Chevy," said Cole, "was an outfit you couldn't get your arms around." He became chief engineer in April, 1952, and his first act was to increase the engineering staff from 850 to 2900. Then he and his team built a brand new V-8 engine, some 40 pounds lighter than the six, with 40 more horsepower. It made all the difference to Chevrolet, and its impact was felt for years to come. As Ed Cole said, "an engine must be made to hang together under any circumstances." Hang together these engines did. For years.

As the reader can see, key men like Sloan, Knudsen, Keating, Curtice, Earl and Cole were all vital to the 1955-57 Chevrolet story. There were many others, of course, and many will be mentioned anon. One could easily dwell upon GM personnel for an eternity. But we digress. Let us consider Chevrolet: what it was, what it became, at the introduction of the revolutionary new 1955 line.

The Chevy was traditionally reasonably priced, reliable, easy to repair, easy to resell. It offered the masses a solid formula of value, comfort and dependability, backed by the strongest, largest and wealthiest dealer network in the world. Being the volume make in the GM hierarchy, Chevrolet probably felt the pain of economic lean years less than its fellow divisions, and to the competition both within and without General Motors, that never seemed fair.

In 1941 Chevrolet, along with other cars, had undergone major body changes. The 1942 facelift was, therefore, minor: a new grille, fenders extending into front doors, the hood lengthened to the door edge, eliminating the side of the cowl. Pearl Harbor came, and with it the stunned realization that America was, once more, involved in a war of global dimensions. In February, 1942, the government put a halt to passenger automobile production, and Chevrolet like all the rest donned olive drab and went into battle.

Chevrolet Division, a winner of the Army-Navy "E" flag for its efforts, supplied 4x4 military trucks, components for 90 mm anti-aircraft guns, and shells of various sizes to the armed forces. It also tooled up for two lines of Pratt & Whitney Aircraft engines, and maintained parts for Chevrolet cars and trucks on the road. It was a distinguished record: eight million shells, 500,000 army cars and trucks, 60,000 Pratt & Whitney engines, 3800 armored cars, two hundred million pounds of aluminum forgings, two billion pounds of gray iron castings. The effort was all-out.

Chevrolet resumed civilian truck production on August 20th, 1945, and car production on October 3rd. The cars were, of course, warmed-over versions of the 1942 models. A GM strike of 119 days, from mid-November to mid-March 1946, put the damper on production and saw Ford outproduce Chevrolet in the abbreviated 1945 period, 34,439 to 12,776.

Management changes were made in June, 1946; M.E. Coyle was replaced as division general manager by Nicholas Dreystadt, formerly general manager of Cadillac. While in the midst of a campaign to increase Chevrolet production, Dreystadt was struck down by cancer in August 1948

Chevrolet resumed civilian automobile and truck production in the fall of 1945, after a four-year pause for World War II.

and replaced by W.E. Armstrong. Illness again struck, and Armstrong had to resign. This loss of managerial continuity slowed down progress, but Thomas H. Keating arrived in 1949 and soon began to take a firm hand over Chevrolet's divisional destiny.

The cars, through 1948, remained prewar in design and engineering, different only through facelifts. All were powered by the "Blue-Flame Six," a durable, unsensational

The 1946 Stylemaster sedan was basically a facelifted 1942.

ohv unit that hadn't seen much revision since 1937: 216.5 cubic inches, 90 horsepower at 3300 rpm. The models were, from lowest-priced up, the Stylemaster, Fleetmaster and Fleetline. Chevrolet soon hit its production stride and was comfortably ahead of Ford for 1946 through 1949, building about 400,000 cars in 1946, 700,000 in 1947, and 775,000 in 1948.

Nineteen forty-nine was a memorable year for all three of the major manufacturers of automobiles, who displayed their first all-new postwar designs. At GM, the redesign had actually begun with the 1948 Cadillac and Oldsmobile, but now it was corporation-wide, with flush front fenders, curved windshields, lower hoods. At Chevrolet, there were fourteen models in two series, the Special and De Luxe, with Fleetline styling (fastback in four body styles) or

Styleline (notchbacks in ten body choices). A new manufacturing plant had opened in Cleveland, and Chevy sales rose to 1,109,958. Only once before had it topped the one million mark, in 1927--the same year Chevrolet was number one for the first time.

This first postwar redesign at Chevrolet was a significant one, for the cars were not to be so totally altered again until that glorious year, 1955. With it were numerous trend-setting features: a lower and longer look achieved mainly through styling (wheelbase of the 1949 was an inch shorter than the 1948), flush front fenders, approaching the height of the hood, more swept-back rear fenders. Headlights, grilles, bumpers and trunks were becoming integrated into the design, instead of being mere add-ons. From an overall view, the 1949 Chevrolet was beautifully executed and smoothly styled. Buyers responded to it, as the sales figures indicate.

People who liked the 1949 couldn't help but approve the 1950 model, because it offered two new features: Powerglide torque converter transmission, giving Chevrolet the first automatic in the low-priced field, and the Bel Air hardtop, the first pillarless model in that field. Powerglide was advertised as convenient, economical and dependable. Coupled to a larger six of 235 cubic inches (3 9/16 by 3 15/16 bore and stroke), it developed 105 bhp at 3600 rpm and provided a little extra power, which the automatic needed. Powerglide was first offered as an option on the De Luxe at extra cost; for those choosing standard shift it was coupled to the older 216.5 cid six with horsepower upped to 92 through slightly higher compression. The wheelbase remained 115 inches.

The Bel Air hardtop gave a valuable "prestige" cachet to this hitherto staid and middle-class automobile, and a definite edge versus Ford and Plymouth. In addition, there were Fleetline or Styleline versions of the Special and De Luxe, 12 body styles in all. The hardtop and Powerglide

Chevy sold nearly 200,000 De Luxe four-doors in 1949.

Emblem of an era: the 1949 De Luxe Styleline convertible.

First Chevrolet hardtop was the 1950 Bel Air, in De Luxe line.

The 1951 De Luxe Styleline four-door sedan, a mild facelift.

added important sales impetus, and calendar year production was a record 1,520,583, up almost 40 percent from the year before. Sales of cars and trucks in the U.S. and Canada also reached a new record, well over two million, the first time any marque had passed this plateau. Those collectors who drive 1949 and 1950 Chevrolets today, and those who remember them when they were contemporary, will strongly echo the validity of the postwar public. One characteristic often mentioned is the car's prevailing feeling of tightness and precision, compared to its Ford and Plymouth competition, the way a gear lever snicked into place, the way a door closed with the solidity of a bank vault. The cars were built as few have been since.

In 1951 Chevrolet necessarily had two tough acts (1949 and 1950) to follow. Changes included a new grille, flush-mounted parking lights, slightly raised rear fenders, miscellaneous trim changes. Bendix brakes replaced Huck units, and the sales brochures called them "Jumbo-Drum," giving the impression that they would stop anything. Engines, however, were the same duo as 1950. Korea was on us, though, and production dropped as Chevrolet signed defense contracts once again. Calendar year output was

Chevy sold close to 100,000 Bel Air coupes in 1953.

1,118,101, well down from 1950 and only 8,000 odd units ahead of 1949.

In December, 1951, GM's Engineering Policy Committee made a significant decision, to "turn Chevrolet around." The goal was attributed to both Harlow Curtice and Charles E. Wilson. It implied a complete alteration of the image, from one of reliable transportation to one of appeal to the youth of the country, to performance instead of dependable-but-conservative transportation. Unfortunately, it would have to wait awhile.

Defense production in 1952 encompassed two million square feet of plant space. Chevrolet built aviation engines mainly, and car production was down to 877,950 for the calendar year. (Ford, too, was well down, at 100,000 units less). But Chevrolet did build its one millionth Powerglide unit in October, 1952, a resounding answer to skeptics who felt automatic in the low price field would not be accepted.

Powerglide, of course, had its detractors, and they were numerous in those years. It's intrinsic to anything new—there are always problems and bugs, and if there aren't, there are those who believe there are. A popular ditty went, "Slip and Slide with Powerglide," and fairly accurately described the slippage common to these early automatics. But many buyers were content to slip and slide, rather than shift for themselves.

Still, the automatic was more expensive to buy, more difficult to work on and, therefore, more expensive to repair. It did lose a degree of control by the driver over the automobile: engine braking in the indirect gears, on which many drivers habitually relied. But it was convenient, and over the years it improved, and the skeptics were gradually silenced.

Nineteen fifty-two, fourth year since the restyle, was a difficult one for Chevrolet saleswise, especially since Ford was out with its second postwar redesign that year. As

Dash proposal by Carl Renner, dated 1952, displays neat rows of instruments, controls, was too expensive for production.

This 1951 Renner concept influenced 1953 Bel Air hardtop.

A 1952 Renner idea for the 1954 car's front end styling.

Another variation on side trim for '53 production program.

Renner suggested 1953 model two-tone, grille, in 1951 art.

Karl Ludvigsen said of the period, "these were practical cars, of almost unrelieved banality. Of the '52 one critic said it 'looked as though it had been designed by Herbert Hoover's haberdasher.' A Chevrolet executive recalled glumly, 'every time a prospective buyer saw one, he thought of his grandmother.' " There were the same old choices, the Bel Air hardtop, the Special and De Luxe, mainly in Styleline guise, as the Fleetline was being phased out, available only in the De Luxe two-door. Engine specifications were unchanged, but engineering personnel were not: Edward N. Cole had come to Chevy from Cadillac, and he soon had that staff of 2900 behind him.

In 1953, the old engine, the "cast iron wonder," began to change. Powerglide-equipped engines had aluminum pistons, new insert-type rod bearings and a more modern pressurized oiling system (standard-shift engines got these in 1954). The aluminum pistons ran the same bore and stroke, but the 216.5 cid engine was no more and the 235.5 dominated the line. With standard shift the six developed 108 hp, its compression up to 7.1:1; with automatic the figures were 115 hp, compression 7.5:1. Ed Cole had rolled up his sleeves.

The 1953 body took on a fairly revised appearance, with a moderately wrapped windshield, no longer divided and, except on low-priced models, a wrapped backlight. Power steering became an option. The model lineup was given a shift, with three series: the One-Fifty, the Two-Ten--and the Bel Air, at Keating's orders a series unto itself for the first time, available as two-door hardtop, two- and four-door sedans, and a convertible. More station wagons were offered (though not in the Bel Air series) at three different prices, and Chevrolet sold 48,654 wagons in 1953, almost four times the 1952 number. The biggest news, though, was America's first mass-produced sports car, the Chevrolet Corvette, available in quantity of 300 for 1953. Its special six offered 150 hp at 4200 rpm,

The first production Corvette, in Polo white, sold for $3250.

achieved via 8:1 compression, and was available only with Powerglide. Using a two-seat fiberglass body, it ran a 102 inch wheelbase and was just 167 inches long. The Corvette, of course, is not part of our major subject; but it is indicative of the new policy then beginning to take effect regarding Chevrolet's image and potential market: the youth sector.

Chevrolet had produced 17 million 105 mm shells before the Korean "emergency" was over, but more important to its minions was the 29th millionth car, which rolled off the line on June 9th, 1953. The 30 millionth followed near the end of the year. Also, Chevrolet became the first to produce over half a million cars with automatic transmission, and all-time Powerglide production passed the 1.5 million mark.

As 1953 had seen fairly extensive restyling, 1954 was of course a minor facelift. Aluminum pistons were an across-the-board feature, however, and horsepower was up to 115 at 3700 rpm on standard shift engines, 125 at 4000 with Powerglide. The same series was retained from 1953, and

Bel Air four-door sedans soon became the best selling models in the Chevy lineup. Above, the offering for model year 1954.

Early Corvette leaves line in Flint; the date: June 30th 1953.

Milestones were recorded by the millions at Chevrolet Division.

a Bel Air station wagon became available. Optional were power brakes, automatic seat and power front window controls. New plants were built in Flint, Tonawanda and Livonia, Michigan, additions made to extant plants in Cleveland, Ohio; Indianapolis and Muncie, Indiana. A completely new line of trucks debuted, with optional 261 cid engines on heavy-duty models.

Chevrolet's fiberglass Corvette was produced in greater numbers for 1954: 3625 for the calendar year, 3640 for the model year. The same body and engine were used as in 1953. Chevrolet's overall calendar year production was 1,414,365, slightly off from 1953, and Ford, which had declared a production blitz that year, was close behind at 1,394,762.

The razzle-dazzle end-of-year selling spree of 1953 was particularly hectic, because more than 500,000 1953 models had yet to be sold industry-wide. Even as late as January 1954, 100,000 of them were left. Sales and produc-

tion were down, *Time* said, "but the output of ill will between car dealers and manufacturers has hit an alltime high." "Bootlegging" reared its ugly head as the most damaging effect of this condition. As the pile-up reoccurred toward the end of the '54 model year, the unsold cars numbered close to 650,000, and overstocked dealers were dumping their 1954s on used car dealers for as much as 25 percent below list. These cars were, in turn, sold by the used-car dealers at near wholesale, undercutting new cars back at the dealerships. The dealers complained that they were being flooded with new cars, the manufacturers felt the dealers were lying down on their job. Dealerships fell like flies: in 1954 1757 of them went out of business, out of 47,000 total. Dealers complained that car prices had risen by 100 percent in the last 14 years, which was not in line with inflationary increases--and even this increase did not reflect the cost of the "optional" equipment becoming desirable on most new cars of the day.

The Ford-Chevy battle played an important part in the new car glut. Ford, determined to overhaul Chevrolet, shoveled cars out of its plants and to its dealers whether they ordered them or not. Chevy responded in kind; during June, 1954, for example, Ford and Chevy cornered 53 percent of total sales, against 37 the previous June.

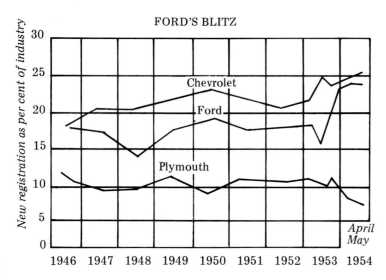

FORD'S BLITZ

New registration as per cent of industry

"When the buyer's market developed in August, 1953, Ford went all out to sell Ford and Mercury. Mercury's bid for place, as sensational as Ford's in 1952, was stopped in its tracks by new 1954 GM Oldsmobiles and Buicks. (Mercury was 'warmed over'). The Ford sales drive gathered momentum during the first five months of 1954 despite Chevy's strong counterattack. In June Ford catapulted to 28.3 percent of the market, with Chevrolet's 25.5 for the month (figures available only in mid-August not shown on the chart). This put Ford 0.3 percent ahead for the first six months of 1954." --William B. Harris in *Fortune*, September 1954.

Dealers resorted to all sorts of gimmicks to rid themselves of the excess cars. One trick was the "special sale," in which toasters, Bermuda junkets, gold watches, or TV sets were offered with every car. Another was "packing prices," whereby the dealer led the customer to believe

that the factory-suggested list price of car and accessories was a lot higher than it really was. Then, said *Fortune*, "he raises the value of the discount (or trade-in) he is offering. Thus a Bel Air convertible that should sell for $2800 gets a $3300 price tag put on it--but screaming banners in the showroom announce that there are $500 discounts for everyone...The upshot is to preserve the car dealer's profit margin while at the same time convincing the poor gull who buys the car that he is getting a special bargain...an eminently idiotic way of doing business [that is] eminently dishonest. Yet one may sympathize to a degree with the dealers who feel obliged to pack their cars. For they are dealing with consumers who have been witnessing price fixing, formal and informal, for many years; and who have, in consequence, got the idea in their heads that the only way to shop is to look for a discount."

Harlow Curtice was one of the first to recognize the potential for disaster in the production blitz and pricing policies, telling dealers that bootlegging was "a malignancy which, if not stopped, will eat away at the very vitals of your business and ours." GM tried persuasion, then put an anti-bootlegging clause into dealer contracts. The Department of Justice said no to the latter, but the House of Representatives passed a dealer-sponsored measure permitting manufacturers to employ anti-bootlegging contracts. The Senate, however, demurred.

It all boiled down to a real dilemma. The fault did not rest entirely with the dealer, nor entirely with the manufacturer. It was one of natural progression. When World War II ended with a seller's market, the industry produced to meet it--but then the industry caught up. Gradually the market turned to a buyer's, culminating in the overage of late 1953 and 1954. Dealers couldn't use prewar hard-sell tactics on a choosey public, now once again firmly in the driver's seat. Manufacturers tried dealer quotas which had no relation to actual dealer needs. Then they tried

The Bel Air convertible for 1954, produced in quantity of 19,333. Top and interior were optionally color coordinated.

exceeding those quotas. It didn't work. Ultimately, the only answer to overproduction was...underproduction. The cuts came.

Meanwhile, who won the production race? As 1955 began *Automotive News* was seen to contain a Ford ad proclaiming Dearborn the winner and new champion, and a GM ad announcing that the title remained safely Chevrolet's. "The Ford car has clinched its position of sales leadership," said Ford Division vice-president Robert S. McNamara. Responded Chevrolet general manager W.E. Fish, "Registrations once again show Chevrolet in first place." Indeed, though the tabulations were in and the dust settled, no one really knew who was the winner.

For the final analysis, R.L. Polk & Company, a firm which sorts and compiles new car registrations, supplied the statistics. "We just supply a service," their spokesmen asserted. "What our clients do with it isn't our business." Polk reported Chevrolet with 1,417,453 cars, and Ford with 1,400,440. Ford protested, insisting that Chevrolet quoted total registration figures to dealers and to the factory, and asked that these cars be deducted from Polk's figures. This gave Ford a net of 1,387,344, Chevrolet 1,362,087. Read that way, Polk made it a Ford year.

This "secondary analysis" by R.L. Polk is usually overlooked in record books today. Other contemporary sources reported other figures, though most of them had Chevrolet ahead of Ford by close to 20,000 cars. Chevrolet rushed the first set of figures to the press agents, noting that they marked "the nineteenth year...the company has consistently held top retail sales honors." Ford took its "secondary" Polk charts and referred only to that "second-place make" which, it said, was reporting only "net regis-

The 1954 Bel Air four-door Townsman wagon saw 8156 copies built.

tration figures." That, one Chevrolet official snapped, was bunk: "We're still the leaders and we defy anyone to tell us differently."

Some of the above may serve to acquaint the reader with the vicious competition going on between Ford and Chevy in those days, and the significance attached to the slightest deviation in sales figures. The Great Race assuredly spurred the Ford-Chevy sales departments like nothing else before or since. From its violent beginning in late 1953, it continued right on through 1957, and anyone who bought a new car during those years could hardly ignore its portent. Plymouth appeared somewhere in the background, a distant third, or worse; it was overwhelmingly a Ford-Chevy battle. The independents, who faced an uncertain future after hasty mergers in 1954, were the real victims of the rivalry. Nash dealers, for example, could not afford to discount and give away cars like those of GM and Ford. To a great extent, the casualties of The Great Race included not Ford or Chevrolet, or Ford Motor or GM, but the independents toward whom the battle was least directed. If Ford did manage to close on Chevro-

let, the latter didn't suffer any severe diminution of sales; rather, Ford was taking sales away from the independents and Chrysler. Chrysler historically took one-fifth of the market; in 1954 it took one-ninth.

Still, one cannot underrate the Ford achievement. Wrote William Harris, "Only eight years ago the principal asset of the Ford Motor Company was its name. Although its properties were large, they were impressive only in size. Buildings were obsolete; machinery was either obsolete or thoroughly worn out. Its principal product, the Ford, was a third-rate car. The company's medium-price motorcar lines, Mercury and Lincoln, could hardly be called competition. In every respect Ford was a poor third to...GM and Chrysler. And it was losing money at the staggering rate of $10 million a month. Ford Motor Company of 1954 is a very different animal..."

Chevrolet faced model year 1955 revived in personnel, confident in its engineering and styling, with its third major postwar restyle and one which, many years later, enthusiasts would hail as its best. If Ford was now closer than before, Chevrolet was more confident than at any time in its recent past it had not only the styling, but the performance to do battle with Dearborn and retain its traditional leadership. Chevrolet waited for the 1955 announcement full of hope for the future.

The rest of the world waited too. Nineteen fifty-five was to be a very important year. During the latter part of 1954, and throughout most of 1955, predictions of car production were found to be 'way below the actual count. It was one of those rare years of almost universal prosperity, and one that would be cited later as one of the great years in the history of the automobile. Chevrolet, as always, would be in there slugging.

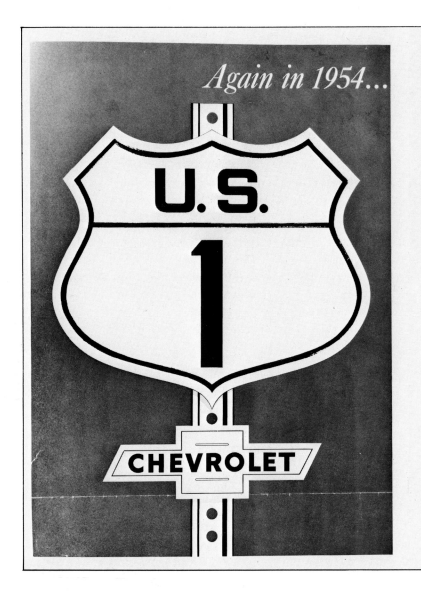

Again in 1954...

for the 19th straight year...

More People Bought CHEVROLETS than any other car!

COMPLETE and official registration figures show that once again—for the nineteenth straight year—Chevrolet outsold all other cars! This great and growing record of sales leadership is a tribute to Chevrolet's unequalled popularity over the years, and to the accomplishments of the most alert and best qualified group of dealers in the automobile business—America's Chevrolet dealers!

In trucks, too, Chevrolet again was first in sales for '54! This is another milestone in Chevrolet's long history of truck leadership—and another record-breaking achievement of Chevrolet dealers.

Already it's clear that 1955, too, promises to be a great year for Chevrolet—and Chevrolet dealers! Chevrolet Motor Division, General Motors Corporation, Detroit 2, Michigan.

America's No. 1 Car!  *America's No. 1 Dealers!*

The 1955 Bel Air sport coupe marked a new era for Chevrolet. It delivered everything the ads promised in beauty and performance.

CHAPTER TWO

1955: Advent of the Hot One

It was a good year, 1955. The cold war was easing, the home economy booming, American fiscal policy on the up-and-up: the estimated federal budget for 1955 saw expenditures of a little over $62 billion, and revenues at $60 billion. Net business income was up 33 percent over 1954, federal employees enjoying a 7.5 percent pay boost, General Motors stock splitting three-for-one. The only check in prosperity came in September, when President Dwight D. Eisenhower suffered a heart attack: the New York Stock Exchange reacted two days later with a $14 billion loss, the heaviest single day's reversal in history.

Progress was being made in health and education: Dr. Jonas Salk announced a successful breakthrough in the search for an antipolio vaccine, racial segregation in U.S. public schools was banned by the Supreme Court. "Cat on a Hot Tin Roof" by Tennessee Williams won the Pulitzer Prize for drama, "The Taft Story" by William S. White was the biographic winner. On Broadway, we watched William Inge's "Bus Stop," listened to the music of S.N. Behrman's "Fanny" and Cole Porter's "Silk Stockings."

At the other end of the musical spectrum the local disc jockey spun such hits as "Rock Around the Clock" by Bill Haley and the Comets, "Sixteen Tons" by Tennessee Ernie Ford and the McGuire Sisters' emotional "Sin--ceer--lee." Davy Crockett fought b'ars and injuns, the Brooklyn Dodgers won their first World Series, Ernest Borgnine starred in the Oscar-winning "Marty." Nashua won the Belmont Stakes and the Preakness, Army beat Navy 14-6, the National League beat the American League 6-5, and Eero Saarinen & Associates won an award from the American Institute of Architecture for the new General Motors Technical Center at Warren, Michigan. It was, almost universally, a vintage twelve months.

Nineteen fifty-five was especially good to the automobile industry. The first eight weeks saw one million cars sold, with GM dealers alone delivering over 450,000 by mid-February. Chrysler sales were up 70 percent over 1954, and Ford was doing well too. As *Ward's* would say later, "In year 1955, the automotive industry exploded." All told, 9,188,574 cars and trucks left the factory, and

Clean '55 grille is now recognized as superior design it was.

the passenger car count was close to eight million. The automobile industry's gross annual product was $11 billion, its total employment roll was 900,000 people, and one out of every six small businesses involved some phase of the car business.

The main reason for these successes was probably the industry's vast array of new products. Ten makes were "all new" in design, seven sporting V-8 engines for the first time--and six of those were brand new engines. The rest were heavily facelifted and boosted in power, as the horsepower race pressed on undiminished. Generally, cars were lower and longer, with bright new colors and color-keyed interiors, tubeless tires, wrap-around windshields and numerous power accessories.

Chrysler Corporation dug in with a vengeance in 1955, after reaching the brink of insolvency the year before. Plymouth and Dodge, pushed far out of competition by the Chevy-Ford battle in 1954, had come back with excellent new styling and new V-8s. Traditionally fine engineering saved the day for Chrysler in 1955, and saw Plymouth come close to doubling its production from the year before.

Tooling up for the greatest across-the-board model change ever, the industry spent $1.3 billion: Ford Division alone spent $185 million for its new body, Chrysler $250 million, Studebaker-Packard $120 million. GM's expansion program was a cool billion, with $300 million earmarked to retool the Pontiac, Oldsmobile, Buick and Cadillac. Another $300 million was set aside just to retool the Chevrolet.

The 1955 Motorama previewed in New York on January 20th as GM led by its indefatigable president Harlow Curtice, flaunted its wares. "He attended an advertising agency party at the Pierre," *Fortune* noted, "...an after-theatre party at the Savoy-Plaza. Tuesday morning he had breakfast with the executives of a steel company to talk them into expanding capacity. At 11:00 A.M. he ran through a TV rehearsal. At noon he held a press conference and hosted a newsmen's luncheon on the Starlight Roof. At four-thirty he was in the receiving line at Vice President Paul Garrett's annual cocktail party at the University Club. At eight he was guest of honor at a publisher's dinner at Mama Leone's. Wednesday morning he hopped over to GM's New York office for a special meeting of the Financial Policy Committee..." And on and on. Even though the New York show was a "killer," *Fortune* said, Curtice continued to perform like duties at other cities on GM's itinerary-- and he filled his off-hours with calls to nearby dealers. By July the show cycle was starting all over again, as preparations for the 1956 Motorama began to be made.

As crowds swarmed into the New York Motorama, they were met by some of GM's most exciting dream cars yet, led by a revived marque, the LaSalle II. Chevrolet showed the XP-37 Biscayne, Pontiac the Strato Star, Buick the Wildcat III, Oldsmobile the Delta, Cadillac the Eldorado Brougham. GMC displayed L'Universelle, on which a distinctive "hardtop" style pillar and roofline could be seen.

It was easy to advertise the '55, new from ground up.

The smartest yet—1955 Chevrolet Bel Air Sport Coupe

Everything's new everywhere you look!

the motoramic

Chevrolet
for '55

New 162-h.p. V8 has 8 to 1 compression ratio— and the shortest stroke in the low-price field.

NEW Show-Car styling—new Sweep-Sight windshield—three new engines ("Turbo-Fire" V8 and two new "Blue-Flame" 6's)—new Glide-Ride front suspension—new outrigger rear springs—new Anti-Dive braking control—new ball-race steering—new 12-volt electrical system — new standard shift transmission or (optional at extra cost) new Overdrive transmission or improved Powerglide, new and improved automatic power helpers.

Chevrolet pulled out all the stops this year, threw every ounce of engineering and production skill into creating a car that is brand-new all the way through. We can't even begin to list all the changes here . . . all the new handling ease, roadability, riding comfort, visibility and wrapped-in-plush luxury. You'll have to drive it to know what the word *new* really can mean . . . when the world's leading manufacturer of cars touches off a revolution! See your Chevrolet dealer for a demonstration. . . . Chevrolet Division of General Motors, Detroit 2, Michigan.

More Than a New Car...a New Concept of Low-Cost Motoring!

Chevrolet Biscayne four-door hardtop was 1955's dream machine.

L'Universelle show van's roof pillar predicted Nomad's coming.

Strayer's City Chevrolet, of Kingston, Pennsylvania, promoted new '55 line with specially decorated "Motoramic Chevy" bus.

At the same show debuted the production versions of the 1954 Motorama Corvette Nomad: Pontiac's Safari and Chevrolet's Nomad--of which much more later. Fifty people per minute inspected the New York show and production cars, and then they did it all over again in Miami, Los Angeles, San Francisco and Boston, total attendance exceeding 2.2 million. The Motorama caravan involved 99 trucks, 1183 crates, 350 full-time employees, and untold carloads of cash--all expended with the goal of convincing the excited attendees to rush right down to their local GM dealership and sign on the dotted line for the car of their dreams. It must have helped, because many people did opt for GM cars in 1955--nearly four million of them. And Chevrolet accounted for nearly half.

What was this 1955 Chevrolet, billed as "The Hot One," the "Motoramic" Chevy, the car with the "New Look, New Life, New Everything" by 7500 dealers around the country, who promoted it with spotlights and flags, banners and salesmen, balloons and pot-holders, perfume and key cases, pencils and beanies? Despite the vulgarity and hoopla, it was quite an automobile. Uncle Tom McCahill of *Mechanix Illustrated*, for example, called it "a junior sized Olds with Buick doors and a Cadillac rear, the most glamorous looking and hottest performing Chevy to come down the pike." Said Walt Woron of *Motor Trend*, "It's sometimes hard to know what to write about first. Should we talk about the car's acceleration, its brakes, its handling? Or discuss its interior, its styling, its ride?" Floyd Clymer of *Popular Mechanics* added, "Best-handling Chevrolet I have ever driven and it feels like a large car." The new Chevy was chosen as pace car for the Indianapolis 500 Mile Race, picked by *Motor Trend* (in a tie with Mercury) as the best handling and most roadable car of the year, even given special mention for outstanding performance and handling by notoriously eyebrow-lifting *Consumer Reports*. Overall, the automotive press conceded that GM had done

what it had set out to do--the Chevrolet image was abruptly, excitingly changed. This was no longer an "old man's car"; it had new styling, new engineering, new performance, new life.

In a talk with Clare MacKichan, head of the Chevy design studio in those days and today executive in charge of advanced engineering, the author asked how GM envisioned the change they'd wrought. "Well, I guess we have to talk a little about Ed Cole," MacKichan began. "He was a very aggressive kind of person. And of course, Harley Earl was pretty aggressive too. We had a pretty good team working for us doing a new kind of car, and I think all the feelings were that the '54 Chevy was sort of old hat, a rather sedate kind of car. We had tried to make it a little different but it really was that kind of car. It had just a straight six engine, and this new V-8 was coming out for 1955. Along with that we all had wanted to do a brand new car and the '55 was new from the ground up. I think everything on it was completely new, right from the tires on."

MacKichan refers, of course, to the December 1951 decision of the GM Engineering Policy Committee to "turn Chevrolet around," which it had begun, as previously mentioned, by bringing Cole in from Cadillac. At the same time, former chief Chevrolet engineer Edward H. Kelley moved over to manufacturing manager--and Kelley worked well with Cole. Harry Barr was brought in from Cadillac as assistant chief engineer, and in this capacity was in charge of chassis and drive train. These and others were assigned the job of producing in little more than two years, an entirely new engine, drivetrain and chassis. It was an impossible task. But it was done.

Shortly after Ed Cole took over as chief engineer of Chevrolet, board chairman Alfred Sloan asked him about his plans. "I just happen to have some plans for expanding Chevrolet engineering," Cole replied, "and I'm ready to show them any time you wish." Sloan waved him on; it

Bel Air convertible was chosen to pace the 1955 Indy 500 race. In view of its new performance abilities, the choice was a good one.

Sauder Chevrolet, New Holland, Pennsylvania, celebrated 25th anniversary with contest which awarded Indy pace car miniatures to lucky winners. In the center are the son and daughter of Freda and Bob Kauffman. Bob, a retired Chevrolet salesman, today owns a '55 Nomad.

Motor engineer Harry F. Barr, with Ed Cole, had enormous influence on 265 V-8.

Edward N. Cole, a major spark-plug as Division manager, and a great engineer.

Edward H. Kelley was Chevrolet Division's chief engineer from 1949 until 1952.

wasn't necessary to show anything. The plans included increasing the engineering crew from 850 to 2900. Quipped Charlie Wilson to Cole, "I'll bet that's the first time you ever had your plans approved without submitting them."

Some of the engineering groundwork had already been laid by Edward Kelley: time had been reserved at Sundstrand, Cross, W.F. & John Barnes, the machine-tool builders, even though Chevrolet had no firm engine design yet. (Engineers were toying with the idea of a V-6 as well as a V-8, and Kelley had a 231 cubic inch V-8 proposal, which was ultimately shelved). Cole had to come up with a firm design in time to use the tool builders' openings. A delay of just a couple of months could easily foul the whole schedule, triggering further delays all the way down the line. When all the development phases were slotted into a time span, Cole found himself with just 15 weeks to design an engine--and he made it, with the aid of Kelley and Barr.

While 15 weeks is enough time to design an engine, it's not usually long enough to insure that the engine will be a good one. That Cole's V-8 proved to be not only good, but great, is a tribute to him and all who worked with him. But to Cole it was as nothing.

"I had worked on V-8 engines all my professional life," Cole later said. "I had lived and breathed engines. Barr and I were always saying how we would do it if we could ever design a new engine. You just *know* you want five main bearings--there's no decision to make. We knew that a certain bore-stroke relationship was the most compact. We knew we'd like a displacement of 265 cubic inches and that automatically established the bore and stroke. And we never changed any of this. We released our engine for tooling direct from the drawing boards--that's how crazy and confident we were."

It should not be assumed that Cole, Kelley and Barr had

an absolutely blank slate, despite the newness of the 265 engine. Though it was a ground up design, there were certain parameters. Since it was intended for Chevrolet, it had to be an "economy engine": cheap to build, efficient in operation. It need not be a poor engine--and it wasn't--

tirely independent of the others, so that deflection of one had no effect on any other. Each was assembled over a valve stem and push rod, retained by a fulcrum ball and lock nut. Regardless of whether mechanical or hydraulic valve lifters were used, the valves were lashed by turning

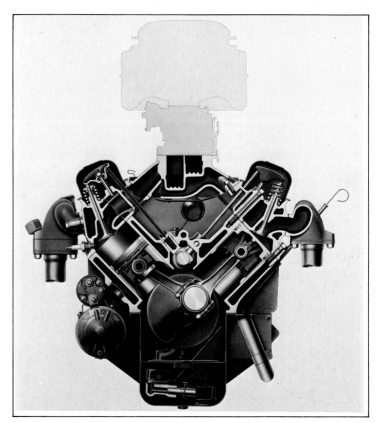

The light and efficient "Turbo-Fire" 162 hp valve-in-head V-8.

Frontal cross section drawing of the "Turbo-Fire" V-8 engine.

but it almost had to be a model of simplicity and economic design--and it was.

One of the outstanding features of the 265 that pointed up how well the engineers had met their goals was the lack of a common rocker arm shaft. Each rocker arm was en-

the lock nut. In addition, the reciprocating weight was reduced, allowing higher rpm, and cutting down on materials. The intake manifold also provided a common water outlet to both heads; and the heads, which were die cast with integral valve guides, were completely interchangeable. The valve train design was shared with that of Pontiac, whose slightly larger V-8 was designed along some of the same principles.

A short stroke engine meant short connecting rods: just 5.7 inches center distance for a stroke ratio of 1.9. Pressed-in piston pins eliminated the slitting of the rod and the need for a locking bolt. Five main bearings of equal diameter carried the maximum loads in their lower halves. "By reducing the maximum oil film loads through omission of the oil groove in the lower half," the *SAE Journal* noted, "the capacity of the main bearings is increased approximately 100%, and wear is reduced."

Further weight saving was accomplished by circulating the oil through hollow pushrods, providing splash lube to the rockers and valve stems instead of using separate and costly oil lines. Three holes, drilled horizontally in the block, provided one main and two tappet oil galleries. A drilled hole from the high pressure main oil gallery lined up with a hole in the camshaft rear bearing shell, maintaining high pressure oil on this bearing steadily, and through another hole to each of the tappet galleries.

Further details included an "autothermic" piston with three rings, a slipper-type aluminum unit with a circumferential expander for the one oil ring, providing axial and radial force to control oil burning. The crankshaft was pressed forged steel instead of alloy iron, because the former had a higher specific gravity and modulus of elasticity, and new forging processes allowed Chevrolet to reduce its overall length. A chart of torsional vibration showed very low peaks without sharp points throughout most of the range; adding a harmonic balancer eliminated remaining torsional vibration.

The exhaust manifolds were routed near the top of the cylinder heads, with exhaust passages pointing upward and out, and the entire length of the ports was water jacketed. "This minimizes the transfer of distortion loads back to the valve seats," the *Journal* noted, "and dissipates heat uniformly from the valve area." Chevrolet switched to a 12-volt electrical system with this engine, as six-volt systems were found unequal to the voltage needs of the high compression powerplant. The 12-volt also provided more efficient generator output, better starting motor operation, and the use of smaller gauge wires and cables.

Because the new engine had better heat rejection than the "Blue Flame Six," a smaller radiator could be used which further reduced rate and frontal radiator area. Overall, of course, the engine itself was lighter than the six:

	V-8	6
Block assembly	147 lbs.	163 lbs.
Cylinder Heads (per engine)	77	72
Crankshaft	47	79
Connecting Rod, Piston, Rings	21	22
Intake Manifold	34	13
Exhaust Manifolds	17	16
Valve Actuating Mechanism	18	25
Total Engine	**531**	**572**

"The whole concept of the car was built around lighter components," Ed Cole reminisced in a 1974 interview with Michael Lamm of *Special-Interest Autos.* "We got away from the heavy torque-tube drive and went to Hotchkiss drive. We went to a Salisbury-type axle instead of the banjo type. Then we went to ball-joint front suspension for weight saving. And we went to a tubular frame [rails]. It was a brand-new engine and a brand-new body, too. Today, if you wanted to take the same sort of risk at Chevrolet, you'd promptly be fired."

Asked if there was any major breakthrough in designing the Chevrolet V-8, Cole said it might have been "when we decided to make the precision cylinder blocks--the heart of the engine--by using an entirely different casting technique. We used the green-sand core for the valley between the

Chassis and running gear of the 1955 Chevrolet, fitted with the six-cylinder engine. Note box girder frame and open driveshaft.

bores. That is, for the 45 degree angle center, 90 degree total, we used a green-sand core to eliminate the dry sand core so that we could turn the block upside down. We cast it upside down so the plate that holds the bore cores could be accurately located. This way we could cast down to 5/32nds jacket walls.

"Now Ed Kelley's background had been heavily oriented toward manufacturing, and anybody who's been in manufacturing has a tendency to design toward what the manufacturing people feel they need. The manufacturing people hadn't been stretched out as much as they could be. For example, when we talked about 5/32nds crankcase

walls, they said, 'Well, you just made a mistake. We don't cast anything less than 5/16ths.' Precision casting was a major breakthrough...I think John Dolza, who was with Engineering Staff, had as much to do with that as anybody, but none of these things are individual ideas. They come out of brainstorming sessions."

In the same interview, Harry Barr pointed out that despite some similarities with Pontiac's V-8, the Chevy had certain advantages. "We knew Pontiac was going on a V-8, and their design was heavier than ours. But they developed a sheet-metal rocker arm that we thought had possibilities. It hadn't been decided yet, but we jumped into that and gave it to our manufacturing group. They determined that they could make stamped rocker arms with no machining whatever--just a metal stamping.

The 1955 "Blue Flame 136" six-cylinder engine produced 136 hp.

"We also lubricated it differently from Pontiac...with the oil coming up through the tappet, up through the hollow pushrod into the rocker arms, then over to lubricate both the ball and the pallet of the rocker arm. The ball was mounted onto a stud that was pressed into the cylinder head. These were all new ideas, and very good as far as automation was concerned. You never had to screw anything--just press these studs in."

Many were responsible for the engine besides the ones we always hear of. "We found a very capable engine designer in Chevrolet--Al Kolbe," Barr continues. "Al had been supervisor of a drafting room and liked management, so he was delighted to become chief designer of this engine.

He had worked on the Packard Twin Six...way back. He was an older man, now deceased. His immediate assistant was Don McPherson, later director of engineering at Chev-

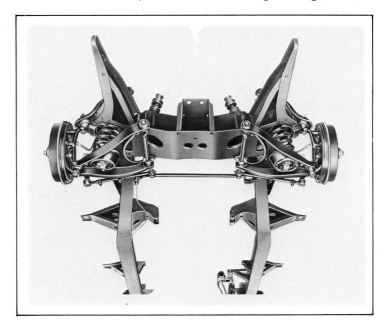

Chevrolet front suspension was responsible for good handling.

rolet. Those two really helped to work with the crew and came up with one of the lightest weight-per-output engines ever."

Aside from the tubular frame rails and Hotchkiss drive, the rest of the mechanical specification was fairly conventional. The independent front suspension consisted of coil springs with coaxial, life-sealed, double-acting shock absorbers, the rear suspension used semi-elliptic leaf springs, 58 inches long by two inches wide and separated by lubrication-eliminating inserts. Rear shocks were diagonal-mounted. The 15-inch wheels ran 6.70x15 four-ply tubeless tires, and the wheelbase was 115 inches. Front track was 58 inches, rear track 58.8. The brakes were self-energizing

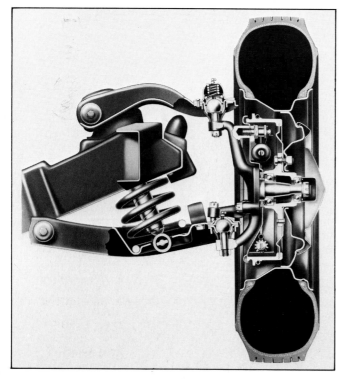

Ball joints, coil springs were used up front...

While "Outrigger" rear springs mounted outside frame at rear.

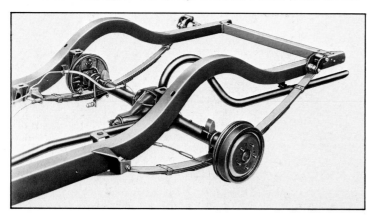

11-inch hydraulic drums, the steering recirculating ball-nut type with a 20:1 ratio. Optional, in addition to Power-glide, was Borg-Warner overdrive--the first appearance of this unit on a GM car.

But the 1955 Chevrolet was a styling sensation as well as an engineering tour de force, and it benefited in this respect from the talents of a man equally as gifted in his field as Ed Cole was in his: Harley Earl. GM's Styling Section readied an all-new body to go with the new engineering of the '55 Chevy, one appropriate to the advances Cole's team had made.

The reader may have an acquaintance with 1955-57 Chevrolet styling already, but after exhaustive research and several interviews, the author has been privileged to appreciate even more the benefits of GM's traditional right moves at the right time. Truthfully, what seemed like a good idea at the time proved through the years to be just that: a design that was balanced, uncomplicated and clean some 20 years later, still quite attractive and still highly appealing to a large body of the collector public. That, coupled with successful engineering, is the reason for Chevrolet's success of 1955-57, and the reason why these cars are so appreciated today.

Harley J. Earl was the Ed Cole of 1955 Chevy styling. The Ferrari-type egg-crate grille, and the notched beltline or beltline dip, for example, were Earl-decreed or instigated. Earl, of course, didn't walk up to a clay model and carve-in these components. Rather they evolved through his well-known process of inspired direction.

"I don't generate all the new forms and treatments," Earl told *The Saturday Evening Post* in 1954. "The whole Styling Section is constantly working on revisions and refinements and totally new lines, and the next one might well come from either a freshman or an old-timer...when I refer to myself I am merely using a short cut to talk about my team. There are 650 of us, and collectively we are known as the Styling Section of General Motors. I happen to be the founder of the Section and the responsible head, but we all contribute to the future appearance of GM automobiles.''

Twenty-two years later, Clare MacKichan echoed Earl's very words, proving the underlying consistency of GM styling philosophy: ''The way the design business works, it is very hard to tell who did what. When you have people working on something in the studio they all come into it to some extent. One person will make a sketch of a car, somebody will make variations, or a completely different one. Out of all that comes a final choice. Plus a few inputs from the boss's own mind.''

Carl H. Renner, a crucial force in the Styling Section during the 1955 Chevrolet program, recently recalled his experiences in literally the same words: ''Although an indi-

Clare MacKichan holds Nomad Club plaque presented to Carl Renner.

Stand a convertible on its tail and you'd have a perfect view of Chevy's strong 1955 X-member frame.

vidual may create a certain design, the total outcome of a product is due to the talent and efforts of many...sometimes one guy creates it, one guy designs it, the other guy supervises it; sometimes one person does all three."

But all sources indicate that the 1955 Chevy's Ferrari-type grille was attribual almost directly to Harley Earl. It was indeed novel for 1955, though its basic design had been seen before--and would be seen again. "Harley Earl was pushing it very hard," said MacKichan, "for the 1955 program. And it was against the wishes, at that time, of the Chevrolet management. He made at least annual trips to Europe, and I guess he had certain ideas of doing it, and he was a fan of European cars for years and years." Says Renner, "Mr. Earl possessed much power. He was the boss. And although some individuals did not agree with his deci-

sions, being boss he had his own way. Needless to say, what he did sold in those years. In the studio, we did our utmost to please him. Although he directed the design of the grille, we designed, illustrated and modeled it, and that was the end result."

The 1955 Chevrolet grille was the source of much controversy. Some dealers didn't like it: those were the days of baudy chromium smiles, full-width expanses of mirror-like bright metal. Ford's grille for 1955 was a concave denture of complex design, though Plymouth's, admittedly, was a simple bar affair. Whether or not a design sells, of course, is unrelated to its intrinsic worth. The 1955 Chevy grille happens to be one of the most elegant components on cars of that era of Detroit manufacture. It was neat, efficient, beautifully simple; it was a great design achieve-

Rare Oldsmobile Fiesta joined limited production Buick Skylark and Cadillac Eldorado as 1953 predictors of 1954-55 styling features.

ment, brought about in spite of overwhelming industry preference for flashier approaches.

The notched beltline, or beltline dip, which appeared for the first time on a Chevrolet in 1955, had actually been introduced on the limited edition Oldsmobile Fiesta, Buick Skylark and Cadillac Eldorado in 1953, and on production versions of those makes in 1954. This too is remembered as an Earl innovation, across-the-boards for GM cars in 1955. "The reason for the break," Clare MacKichan told us, "was something again that Harley Earl inspired. He liked low roofs--that is why you see thick sheet metal. He liked low windows--none of these cars have very huge windows, like you see on the road today. He liked very low rear quarters, so to get that feeling he wanted to raise the rear fender, and sometimes it was higher than the beltline at this point. That is how we got into that kind of dipped shape."

The location of the notch on the beltline was a particular problem. C.A. Stebbins, chief designer of body development during those years, recalls how that final decision was reached: "The four-door sedan was modeled and approved first, and always had some type of dip in the belt profile. For many weeks, the clay model had front fenders higher than the hood, the belt tailing down an inch or so in the area of the front door, breaking and sweeping back in one line to the taillamp. The point of intersection, where the dip terminated, was constantly in flux, with Mr. Earl seemingly unable to agree exactly where it should occur. This factor, plus the high front fender profile, was resolved one morning when Mr. Earl decreed that the fenders should be cut down and the dip moved back onto the rear door resulting in the final belt design." Once that decision was made, placement of chrome molding outlining the two-toning treatment, which was dependent upon the placement of the notch, could be finalized.

Carl Renner points out that Earl's stature had a good

Charles Stebbins, chief designer, body development in 1955.

deal to do with his vision of things. "He was six foot four," Renner remembers, "and mock-ups looked quite different than they would to an average-sized person. Therefore, on-the-job designers, in order to view their efforts as Earl did, strapped blocks of wood to their shoes, which afforded them the same vantage point--all unknown to Mr. Earl, of course."

Granted Earl's significant role in the grille and notched beltline, these were simply two details involved in a basic form already established and nearly-finalized in clay. But where did *that* come from? The answer requires a look back a few years at the evolution of Chevrolet styling and the direction of Harley Earl's stylists.

The first three major postwar styling changes for Chevrolet occurred in 1949, 1953 and 1955. While the public

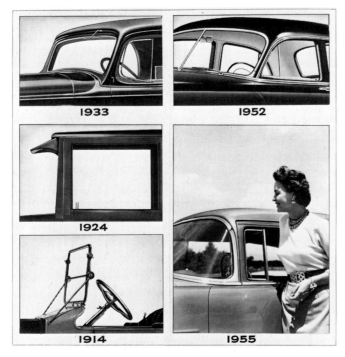

A Chevy composite traces development of windshield from 1914.

witnessed the advent of the Bel Air sport coupe in 1950 and the disappearance of the fastback Fleetline model by 1953, Earl's Styling Section was busily at work, sketching dreams on sheets of paper, modeling them into clay, watching them become reality for the 1953 to 1957 program,

and even beyond. Some of those dreams, however, remained just that, dreams...pieces that did not fit into the final program. Nevertheless, they were a major part of Earl's comprehensive styling philosophy: "go all the way and then back off," which, more often than not, led to the finalization of a basically balanced design.

The paramount theme continued to be "lower, longer and wider," if not always in reality, at least visually. Windshields, no longer divided by 1953, were starting to wrap around, as were rear windows. Consequently, the configurations of the A and C pillars were revised, particularly in coupe models. Fenders were approaching the level of hoods and decks, this manifested either by raising them, lowering hoods and decks, or a combination of both. Earl's stylists even experimented with the hood sunken *lower* than the fenders, according to chief of body development C.A. Stebbins, but this was abandoned: from a frontal view the upper body appeared too tall, and engineering-wise it wasn't practical. With regard to contour, Chevrolet's front fenders had become flush with the body by 1949. Elsewhere in the industry rear fenders as well had become integral, as did Chevrolet's by 1955.

Body side innovations also occurred. Previously, Chevrolet two-toning was delineated by the beltline: the upper body one color, the lower body another. On the new top-of-the-line Bel Air series for 1953, Chevrolet stylists introduced a lower body horizontal color flash along the fender sculpturing above the wheel cutout, and outlined it in trim molding. This tended to attract the viewer's eye downward, thus providing a lower longer look.

This treatment was continued in the 1954 model, but on the 1955 Bel Air it took on more daring dimensions, for one of the two-tone options included a roof, rear deck and upper rear quarter of one color, separated from the rest of the body color by a stainless steel molding. Along

Renderings by Carl Renner. Above left, the 1955-57 bumper and greenhouse emerges, 1952; right, the egg crate grille circa 1952.

Above, 1953 rendering suggests bumper-grille, slotted hood; right, a Renner sketch shows early wrapped backlight, as drawn in 1951.

with the appearance of lower body two-toning, designers began experimenting with notched beltlines, sheet metal crossovers and sweepdowns which were contingent upon chrome moldings, body sculpturing or both. Aesthetically, this all affected wheel cut openings and rear fender endings.

Hooded headlamps and hooded fenders were developed. Between them were grilles expanded into wider proportions with parking lamps placed outboard.

In November, 1954 *Time* featured the 1955 Chevrolet, referring to an early clay model which wore a horizontal crease in the molding of the trunk. Harlow Curtice, *Time* wrote, "circled the car, squinting at its lines and lightly touching its smooth surface. When his eye lighted on a horizontal crease in the molding of the trunk, he shook his head. 'That's not good,' said Curtice. 'You'll see that it casts a shadow on the bottom half of the lid. That shadow makes the car look higher and narrower. What we want is a lower automobile that looks wider.' "

On this point the author asked C.A. Stebbins for his recollections: "In recalling the development of the deck crease on the 1955 Chevrolet, my original suggestion was accepted by Harley Earl, and the clay model was sculptured as shown on the enclosed sketch. [See color section.]

"Ed Cole, the new chief engineer of Chevrolet, very much liked the idea. At the time of the first 'final' showing of the clay in the auditorium of the Styling Section, however, the crease had been removed at Mr. Earl's request. Cole asked to have it reinstated, whereupon Mr. Earl replied that we would make the fiberglass model with the deck both ways so that '...you can have another look at it.' This was never done."

Stebbins continued: "At the time, the idea was quite 'far out,' never having been done before. In any case, it had failed to sufficiently enchant Mr. Earl. But contrary to the *Time* magazine description, the effect of the deck crease would have been to widen and lower the appearance of the rear of the car." But what is perhaps most important is that Stebbins' clean taillamp treatment was approved and incorporated into the final Chevy body. Its simplicity and balance of design has survived two decades, wearing as well today as it did originally.

Graphics, front, side and rear, was the game Harley Earl was playing, and his inspired stylists were a formidable team. Carl Renner shared with the author a vignette which best explains the talent Harley Earl possessed. Prior to beginning work in the GM Styling Section in 1945 at age 22, Carl held his first job with Walt Disney Studios, where he churned out animations of Disney characters for approximately two years. He spoke of Disney's talent for incorporating the best contributions of his artists: "He had an uncanny ability of combining just the right things...of directing us, of inspiring us...selecting the proper nose, which went with the most suitable ears, and just the right mouth." Relating Disney to Harley Earl, Carl then spoke of the latter: "He was a terrific man, with the ability to guide people into things...we had six designers sitting there and everyone had the opportunity to express himself, and the one main objective was to sell your creativity to these people. That was the method of operation at that time. Also, you had your own niche, and you could decorate your work area the way you liked with pictures of pin-up girls, your favorite designs, cars or whatever inspired you. This somewhat reflected you, and people knew what you stood for."

As Disney is remembered for his major contributions to the world of cartoons over many years, so Harley Earl should be remembered for his influence on many, many automobiles for over three decades. The longevity of his rule, the Motorama shows, his expert touch on the first Corvette, the "Corvette Nomad" and the 1955 Chevrolet, were all of major importance to General Motors in the highly competitive middle Fifties.

The 1955 Chevrolet was available in three series; the One-Fifty, the Two-Ten and the Bel Air. The same three series were offered in 1954, but that's where the similarity ended. One had a choice of 16 different body styles* and nine power teams** and an array of bright, bold colors, especially conceived for two-toning.

"HERE'S CHEVROLET'S NEW 'SHOW CAR' STYLING AT ITS BEAUTIFUL BEST" shouted sales brochures. "NEW LOOK! NEW LIFE! NEW EVERYTHING!" The new look appeared two and one half inches lower (wagons were up to six inches lower), a "Sweep-Sight" windshield wrapped around, increasing front seat visibility by 19 percent, and the backlight wrapped --the latter was a startling change on the station wagon line. Four-door sedans now boasted 3528 square inches of glass area. From the driver's seat all four fenders were visible, with hood, belt, and deck lines considerably lower than in 1954. The driver faced a completely redesigned twin cowl dash and instrument panel, (that design being first seen in the Motorama Corvette in 1953), which contoured to the shape of the windshield; gearshift concentric with the steering column; and a recessed hub steering wheel. Decorating the Bel Air dash were 987 "bow ties," Chevrolet's official logo, the design idea developed by Carl Renner, reproduced en masse as a constant reminder one was behind the wheel of a Chevrolet. Renner's hood "bird" became another Chevrolet trademark: he had designed hood ornaments from 1953 through 1956.

The overall shape of the 1955 Chevrolet was a complete departure from 1954. It was boxy, yet aesthetically taste-

* The Bel Air two door Nomad station wagon was added to the line in February, 1955. The Two-Ten sport coupe was added in June, 1955.

** Original choice of power teams was six. Later 180 hp 4-barrel version available with 3-speed, overdrive or Powerglide increased choice to nine.

Details of the 1955s: Left, the suspended brake pedal and villainous air vent. Center, the dash with bow-tie perforations, and cowl-mounted air scoops. Below, the Renner-designed hood bird and a wide-angle view of the Chevrolet grille —held, at least in retrospect, as its most distinguishing feature.

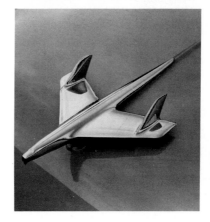

Cameo Carrier was the name given to 1955's clean pick-up truck.

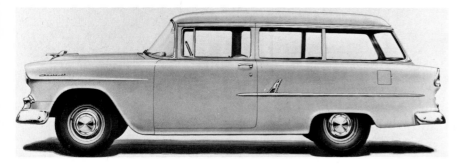

The 1955 Two-Ten two-door wagon, production 29,918, cost $2178.

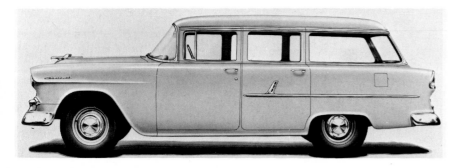

Four-door version saw 82,303 units built, was priced at $2226.

ful, thoroughly integrated and balanced, and wore its new two-toning options quite well. It made sense from the no-nonsense "Ferrari" style grille to the attractively simple taillight treatment.

Interior and exterior trim differed in the three series, though any power team was available with any body style. The bottom line One-Fifty came as both a two- and four-door sedan and a two-door utility sedan; the seatless rear compartment of the latter could be used for hauling cargo as the floor was raised for easier loading and unloading. Also offered was a two-door Handyman station wagon with an all vinyl interior. (Though not part of the passenger line, a sedan delivery came with One-Fifty trim).

Interiors were stripped spartan, with rubber mats covering the floor rather than carpets. Seat and door panel material was unglamorous though practical. Body side treatment for the One-Fifty was noticeably "plain Jane" with no chrome at all, except for a lonely Chevrolet script on the front fender, a touch of chrome on the door handle and bumper chrome wrapped around at either extremity. Windshields and backlights, as well as beltlines and roof edges, were untrimmed. For $1593, though, you could have a brand-new 1955 six-cylinder Chevrolet. Undressed, and a far cry from the V-8 equipped two-door Bel Air Nomad station wagon at $1000 more, it was an excellent value for money.

Two-Tens were available in six choices: two- and four-door sedans; Delray club coupe; sport coupe (added to the line in June 1955); and a pair of station wagons (two-door Handyman and four-door Townsman). The Delray was advertised as a combination of the style and roominess of a two-door sedan with a custom two-tone vinyl interior. The mid-year addition of a two-door sport coupe, the same body as the Bel Air in Two-Ten trim, was prompted by sales of the Bel Air and Delray coupes (year end production 185,562 and 115,584 respectively). Unfortunately,

A pair of sedans: left, the obviously popular Bel Air four-door ($2031 and best-selling model); right, the Two-Ten variation.

its late introduction and other factors resulted in low production at 11,675.

For the extra money, the Two-Ten line was a sensible investment over the One-Fifty. Exterior trim included stainless steel around windshield and backlight, as well as on the beltline. A chrome Chevrolet script appeared on the front fender, and a pair of bright moldings, running down from the rear side window and forward from the rear fender, set off the after end of the car. This treatment not only drew attention to the beltline notch but accentuated the integral fender styling.

The wagon body did not have a beltline dip. Both two- and four-door wagons were therefore enhanced by the horizontal trim strip with its leading edge topped by a winged spear, reaching diagonally back toward the straight beltline. Other niceties, absent on the One-Fifty but standard on the Two-Ten, included chrome front seat and sidewall moldings, a glove compartment light, an ash receptacle, a cigarette lighter, arm rests and assist straps.

Among the 1955 Chevrolets the Bel Air, that prestigious French terminology meaning "beautiful line," was simply that. What had originated in 1950 as a sporty, youthful image car, the singular Bel Air hardtop, had by 1953 been stretched into an entire series. It appeared in 1955 lavished with notable visual distinction.

The Bel Air series included six choices: two- and four-door sedans, sport coupe (hardtop), convertible, a four-door station wagon and a February 1955 introduction, the two-door hardtop styled Nomad. The four-door sedan was Chevy's bread-and-butter model with 345,372 Bel Air versions produced. Coupled with the four-door Two-Tens, these accounted for over one third of total production. The handsome Bel Air sport coupe had a chrome ribbed vinyl headliner and optional two-toning that made it much more attractive than in 1954, and its 1955 sales surpassed those of the two-door sedan. Chevrolet's Bel Air convertible made a startling impression as sales more than doubled those of 1954 (41,292 versus 19,333). Station wagons were enjoying a tremendous increase in popularity, and sales almost tripled from 1954 (161,856 versus 56,735), though three times as many Two-Ten wagons were sold compared to Bel Air wagons.

BLUE-RIBBON BEAUTY

that's stealing the thunder

from the high-priced cars!

Wherever outstanding cars are judged . . . for elegance, for comfort, for beauty of line and excellence of design . . . a surprising thing is happening. The spotlight is focusing on the new Chevrolets with Body by Fisher! Surprising—because Chevrolet offers one of America's lowest-priced lines of cars. But not really astonishing when you consider that its team of internationally famous engineers and stylists spent three years creating the 1955 models, and that they had just one goal—to shatter all previous ideas about what a low-priced car could be and do.

The unparalleled manufacturing efficiency of Chevrolet and General Motors provided the means—and that's why you have a low-priced car that looks like a custom creation,

from the crisp, clean grille to the high-poised taillights, from the tubeless tires to the broad crystal arc of the Sweep-Sight windshield. That's why you get the thistledown softness of Glide-Ride front suspension—but married to the sports-car stability of outrigger rear springs. That's why you can choose between a hyper-efficient 162-h.p. V8 engine, with the shortest stroke in its field, or two brilliant new 6's. That's why Chevrolet's array of extra-cost options includes every luxury you might want—Powerglide, Overdrive, Power Brakes and Steering, even Air Conditioning on V8 models. And that's why you should try a Chevrolet for the biggest surprise of your motoring life! . . . Chevrolet Division of General Motors, Detroit 2, Michigan.

See and drive the motoramic Chevrolet at your Chevrolet dealer's!

THE FRENCH HAVE A PHRASE FOR IT: "Concours d'Elegance"—a competition in automotive style and luxury. Here, against the background of a "concours" at California's fashionable Pebble Beach, is the new Chevrolet Convertible—a car that fully reflects, in line and spirit, the great tradition of custom car design.

Chevy was "stealing the thunder" from pretentious contemporaries, according to '55 ads. The Rolls in the background is prominent...

The origin and story of the 1955 Chevrolet Bel Air Nomad station wagon will be dealt with in a separate chapter. Even though it was a part of the 1955 line, it shared almost no sheet metal back of the cowl with the rest of the '55 line. It certainly had little to do with putting Chevrolet in the number one position that year as production fig-

ures were the lowest of all models at 8,530 (.0046 percent of total production).

There was considerably more exterior trim on the Bel Air series than on the Two-Ten. The overall effect was best described by *Motorsport's* Bill Callahan and Bill Schroeder who that year called the 1955 Bel Air sport

The Bel Air Beauville four-door wagon was priced at only $2361...

While the Bel Air sport coupe (production 185,562) cost $2166.

Traditional line leader was the convertible. Offered in the Bel Air series only, over 41,000 were built. The price was just over $2300.

A two-door sedan's rear quarter panel is fitted during 1955 body assembly at Detroit, using jigs, welders, mechanical assistance.

Further along the same production line, a sedan roof is mated to a body and cowl assembly by a pair of workers.

coupe "the number one design in the low-priced field as well as the best design of the year. Restrained use of [brightwork] frames what is probably the best two-tone color separation seen this year."

The Chevrolet script adorning the front fender of both the One-Fifty and Two-Ten series was replaced by a horizontal strip running from behind the headlight back onto the door, slightly higher than the rear molding. Its placement was not happenstance: it carried through the hooded fender contour, and complimented the rear quarter trim.* Stainless steel trim appeared above the side windows, in addition to the same garnishings as the Two-Ten series. Full wheel covers enhanced optional wide whitewalls (Goodrich or U.S. Royal), and the entire line took on a visual prestige unknown before 1955. Particularly important were the optional two-toning treatments which were contingent upon body style. One had a choice of roof only, or roof, rear deck and upper rear quarter in a contrasting color. The latter was particularly striking on the sport coupe, as well as the convertible, with the soft top and boot matching the deck color.

Inside, the Bel Air was equally well appointed with carpeting replacing rubber mats. Possibly impractical was the inclusion of carpeting on the floor of the convertible. Dressier materials, patterned cloth, gabardine and vinyl were available.

The line-up of Chevrolets for 1955 was an impressive package, from the austere utility sedan to the classy convertible. But the biggest bonus was under the skin: Chevrolet's new V-8 engine, which represented a dramatic change in the character of the marque. Happily, the V-8 cost only $99 more than the six, and was available in any

* This trim differed from the Two-Ten in that the horizontal strip was wider, and carried a narrow insert of white paint within its confines. Above this, behind the angle formed by the rear side molding, appeared the Bel Air script and golden Chevrolet crest.

model from the handsome Bel Air to the plain brown wrapper One-Fifty.

Actually, this was Chevrolet's second V-8--the first had been an unsuccessful engine built back in 1917. The '55 was anything but unsuccessful: an overhead valve, high-performance, lightweight, oversquare design (3.75x 3 inches bore and stroke), it was efficient, economical and powerful. No less than 43 percent of 1955 Chevrolet buyers opted for it, and those who didn't had an improved six, with 123 horsepower or 136 with Powerglide. Both engines were available with optional ($108) "Touch-Down" overdrive, which cut in above 31 mph, reducing engine speed 22 percent. But the V-8 was the major attraction. Even though its presence was signified only by small "V" decorations below the taillights, and on the steering wheel hub, a nudge of the accelerator was all the driver needed to remind himself that Chevy performance had arrived.

The V-8's rise in popularity had been sudden. In 1950 it had held only 26 percent of the market; in 1953 it was up to 38 percent and in 1954 it passed 50 percent. In 1955, with both Chevrolet and Plymouth introducing new V-8s, and others springing up all over the industry, fully 78 percent of new cars were V-8 powered.

The 265 cubic inch Chevrolet V-8 delivered 162 hp at 4400 rpm, though a "power-pack" (four-barrel Rochester carburetor and dual exhausts, except station wagons) brought it to 180 hp at 4600 rpm. Axle ratios were 3.70:1 with the manual gearbox, 4.11:1 with overdrive and 3.55:1 with Powerglide.

The lusty new engine allowed Chevrolet to add air conditioning to its option lineup for the first time in 1955. Though expensive at $565, it could be had in all V-8 models except the convertible. Brochures described it as "combining heating and cooling in one highly efficient unit...the whole thing fits compactly into the front of the car [and] requires no trunk space."

Hardtop competitors: the 1955 Bel Air...

The 1955 Ford Crown Victoria...

The 1955 Plymouth Belvedere V-8.

At $565 air conditioning was a costly option, not often seen.

Other optional equipment installed at the factory included power steering ($92), power brakes ($38), power front seats and windows ($145). Power steering had been available since 1953, but because of Chevrolet's new steering linkage the 1955s could be fitted with an improved version priced more economically and easier to service. "Pivot-pedal power brakes," a tongue twister thought up by the ad men, "still retain the familiar feel of complete stopping control," whatever that meant. "A vacuum power cylinder supplies added power which exerts pressure on the car's hydraulic braking system. A reserve tank assures a vacuum reserve even when the engine is not running."

Minor accessories for 1955 were many and varied. There was a vanity mirror for the sun visor, an electric shaver, a chrome-plated tissue dispenser. And, for $123, the buyer

Right: the Chevy V-8 was set well back for optimum weight balance, yet it remained easily accessible for most mechanical operations. Below, the 1955 Corvette, which took a back seat to the passenger car line in 1955 promotion, and sold for $2934.

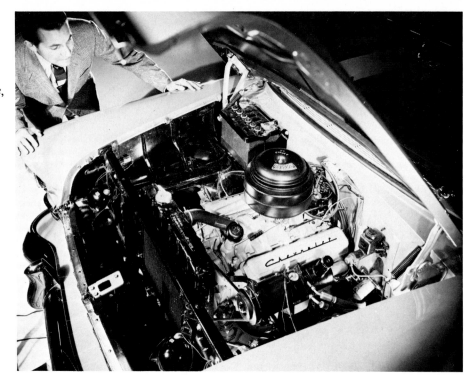

could specify the famed "Wheel Carrier Continental."

Thinking back to those new beauties in mid-Fifties "Easter-egg" hues of Coral, Dusk-rose, Regal turquoise and Skyline blue, it seems like only yesterday that we were reading the bubbly road tests. What was it really like to live with the car as Floyd Clymer did, reporting for *Popular Mechanics*, on a 992-mile drive in a four-door Bel Air through the Mojave desert, Arizona and Nevada? Or Walt Woron, editor of *Motor Trend*, who was continually hopping into another '55 for an updated report?

They all liked the styling, McCahill especially: "It has the best of the General Motors look." Walt Woron admired the quality of exterior workmanship--"The panels all seem to fit fairly well, there aren't any ripples in the body, there's only the barest amount of orange peel in the paint" --but he thought the new egg-crate grille would be a devil to take care of: "Looks like you'll need a bottle brush to keep each square clean." That wasn't far from wrong, as owners found out. Fifteen percent of Floyd Clymer's Chevrolet owners polled felt the grille should be changed. It ranked third highest on the complaint list.

But behind that grille was a masterfully accessible engine compartment which had the generator right out in front on top. Upon removing the air cleaner, both the carburetor and distributor were in plain view. Woron noted, "the fuel pump is low, but you can get to it and work around it. The oil dipstick isn't hard to reach, and oil filling (for you home mechanics) is a cinch." The battery was handily reached, but changing spark plugs was a bugaboo. They were located under the exhaust manifolds, not the things to remove while the engine was still hot.

Even the trunk received favorable comment. Its 20 cubic foot capacity prompted Tom McCahill to stuff it with his hunting buddy--six foot four, 250 pound Jim McMichael --capture the sight with his lens, and publish it in the Feb-ruary 1955 issue of *Mechanix Illustrated*. Later, McCahill claimed that the '55 station wagon was "large enough to carry a troop of polar bears, Jim McMichael and a scale model of Mount Vesuvius."

Behind the wheel of the Chevy, visibility was excellent. All four fenders were in sight, and the "Sweep-Sight" windshield and wrap-around backlight were a substantial improvement over 1954 models. Woron picked up a slight amount of distortion at the far side of the windshield, but praised the windshield wipers which reached previously unswept areas on GM cars. Unfortunately, the narrow limitations of the inside rearview mirror did not reflect the full panorama of the wraparound backlight. Clymer and Woron approved of the easy-to-read fan-shaped speedometer, but disapproved of the way the full-circle horn ring blocked part of its readings.

Oil and generator gauges, stricken from the dash panel in 1955, were replaced by red warning lights which were not a popular innovation. Said Clymer, "The amount of oil pressure and generator output is unknown...lights now notify the driver only when they drop to zero. I prefer gauges that tell what is happening as well as what is not."

There were mixed emotions regarding comfort and convenience of driving position, with *Consumer Reports* claiming, "short drivers will find the steering wheel rim too high for comfortable vision." One Tennessee service rep, who was probably short *and fat*, felt "the steering wheel should be close to dash; short-legged person finds it too close to stomach." But Clymer liked its placement: "Driving position is excellent as is the angle of the steering wheel."

Chevy's front bench seat, described by Woron as "fairly soft, yet firm enough not to be tiring on long trips" was the same seat that *CU* called "low and not very soft," and Clymer thought "should have more padding and better

Rear passenger compartment of the 1955 Bel Air four-door.

springing." Even though the front seat adjusted easily enough on its track, there was not enough movement rearward (4.4 inches) for tall, long-legged drivers. There was plenty of head room and shoulder room in the back seat, and safety was a feature with the front seat-back springs covered, preventing skinned shins. Push-down buttons on rear door locks were another safety feature.

How did it handle? What was the reason behind *Motor Trend's* awards for "best handling" and "most roadable"

(tied with Mercury), or *Consumer Reports'* special mention for handling in its price class? *Motor Trend* pronounced: "...That mushy feeling, so long associated with the American automobile, is gone. In its place is beginning to emerge a feeling of solid sureness, a willingness to be steered, not aimed. These are all heartening characteristics..."

Woron wrote authoritatively about handling: "We didn't have to correct the wheel on a straight road unless there was a crown...easy to steer, even with our fingers (and this wasn't a power-steering car)...when we deliberately drove it off the shoulder the car would move aside, but wouldn't whip so as to cause us to lose control...the same thing happened on street-car tracks and ruts.

"When we took it intentionally too fast through corners, all four wheels would drift, indicating understeer. We made the rear end break loose, but only by hitting the brakes hard, locking the wheels, forcing it to start spinning. Even before we applied more power, we could correct its slide by turning into it. Taking one foot off the brake and then punching the throttle brought it completely out of the spin. This, and whipping the steering when we were going down a road at 55 mph, allowing the car then to seek its own straight course, indicates good inherent front end stability.

"...There wasn't any wheel vibration until we started over rough roads. We could throw it into corners at practically any speed...even through turns that would make most other cars quail..."

Consumer Reports echoed those sentiments but did complain that "the amount of steering-wheel winding required is just below the maximum which *CU* regards as tolerable." (Small turn-circle diameter, 38 ft. curb to curb, 41 ft. wall to wall, with 5½ turns from lock to lock.) It also experienced difficulties with the brakes on three test Chevrolets which were judged erratic, "sometimes pulling

Typically two-toned, the 1955 Bel Air convertible complete with passengers in the mid-Fifties idiom, a publicity broadside.

to one side or the other...though they were of more than adequate power...making swerving rather than straight stops." However, *MT*-prepared road tests of Chevrolets rated their braking capacity superior to Ford and Plymouth. In its award to Chevrolet and Mercury *Motor Trend* drew the following comparison: "Brakes on both cars are good, with Chevrolet having a slight edge." Woron's road test of the '55 Chevy attested that: "The brakes perform as they should in a car like this. Stopping distances are less than those required for the '54. In making panic stops from 60 mph, with all wheels locked, it kept a straight course, beginning to swerve only at the very end (when it's easy to control.)" Perhaps that's where *CU* had trouble.

In addition to the characteristics of handling (roadability) and performance, a car is judged for its "riding qualities." It is perhaps the toughest one upon which to pass judgement because it is something of a personal choice and falls in the area defined by *Motor Life* as: "a necessary compromise between soft, comfortable ride and a suspension firm enough to get you through corners," or what Woron spoke of as "a ride not being sacrificed on the altar of roadability" or vice-versa.

Popular Mechanics' Chevy owners poll rated Chevy's ride below performance and handling, as seen in the following chart:

Best-Liked Features

V-8 Owners

Power, performance	50%
Exterior styling	35%
Handling ease	30%
Riding comfort	21%
Visibility	19%

In the final analysis, the Chevrolet ride was firm, with major emphasis upon handling. For those who wanted "living room" comfort, it probably seemed hard. For those who paid more attention to handling, it was just right.

But no one disputed Chevrolet's V-8 performance. We can dwell upon it six ways to Sunday; it still comes out on top every time.

Floyd Clymer put a 162 hp Bel Air with Powerglide through a 1000-mile test and noted that it cruised at 90 and would top 108, but that one did pay for this performance with regard to fuel economy. The 1953 Chevy, for example, had returned 19.4 miles per gallon on Clymer's test; the new V-8 scored 16.1. *Motor Trend*, however, drew 21.9 mpg with a 1955 six, 2 mpg better than the six for 1953.

Powerglide, especially when hooked to the V-8, also came in for strong praise, especially by *Motor Trend*. "Can you imagine a Chevy being able to stay with a Chrysler, Lincoln, and Oldsmobile?" questioned Woron. "We couldn't believe it either [but] the bank of stopwatches just doesn't lie...The automatic upshift, even under full throttle, is smooth, while downshifts are practically unnoticeable. To downshift manually, you can move the lever to low, but it won't go into that gear until the speed has dropped to approximately 55 mph (as a protection against over-revving). At any speed under 55 mph, shoving the throttle all the way to the floorboard will downshift the transmission to low, giving you a terrific boot. The Powerglide in this car is much quieter than that of the '54 Chevy."

If the basic V-8 was a potent performer, the 180 hp version had to be quite mind-boggling, and *Motor Trend* was quick to borrow one for a road test. The following comparisons were posted, using fifth wheel measurement:

Speed or Distance	Stock Chevy	180-hp Chevy	1954 Cadillac	1954 Buick
0-60	12.3	11.4	11.3	12.1
¼-mile	19.0	18.4	18.4	17.9
30-50	4.4	4.2	5.7	5.2
50-80	15.5	12.9	12.7	13.6

Commented Woron: "The 0 to 60 was made using low range only; using drive gave me a time of 12.8. In the quarter-mile I stayed in low until 60, then shifted to drive: using drive alone gave a slower time of 18.8. The 30 to 50 time was made in low; in drive I got 5.9. In the 50 to 80 run I kept it in low to 60 mph, then upshifted; straight drive time was 13.5."

Meanwhile, *Road & Track* testers jumped into a 180 hp Two-Ten two-door with standard shift and overdrive 4.11 rear axle, to better Woron's 0-60 time by a little under two seconds (9.7) and cut a full second off his standing quarter-mile (17.4). Interestingly, overdrive wasn't a determining factor as the '55 turned a higher top speed in direct drive, refuting Woron's premise that overdrive times would be lower. What it did prove was that manual shift times were better than Powerglide manual shifts from low to drive.

Fifty-five Chevys did have some early problems which is *de rigueur* for any new engineering design. Wrote *Consumer Reports*, "Questionable was the high oil consumption encountered in *CU*'s car; whether this was part of the break-in process or chronic fault will be ascertained by future tests and by owners' reports."

Sure enough. An Ohio shipping clerk told Clymer, "To begin with, it used about three quarts of oil every ten days, but after 1000 miles it dropped to two quarts. Now it's only one quart." Clymer himself noticed high consumption in his road test, two quarts in 400 miles. He requested Chevrolet Engineering make a statement of explanation, which was published in part in March, 1955.

Said W.R. Mackenzie, Division Liaison Engineer, "The figure of 22 percent of owners complaining that the V-8 uses too much oil is very unrealistic at this time. It is true that we have experienced some problem with the oil consumption on the very first engines. This was due in part to the chrome oil-ring installation which was slow to break in and in part to a greater oil supply to the valve operating mechanism than was planned. Both of these conditions were corrected very early and the 22-percent figure becomes less realistic every day. Only the first, relatively few, engines gave trouble.

"With the new ring we are showing oil economies so good that we hesitate to quote them here. We are well satisfied that this problem is well in hand and our service department, working through the dealers, will take care of any owner's problem by first installing the new oil deflector, then if this is not effective, the new rings--on the early engines, of course, they did not have the rings.

"The slow seating of the chrome rings has its good returns, generally speaking, in long life and outstanding oil economy after they are properly seated."

Another weakness in early Chevys surfaced in *MT*'s gossip column, "The Rumor Mill," in early 1955. Rumor: "Both Pontiac and Chevrolet experiencing excessive service problems with new V-8s, specifically failure of 'stamped' rocker arms." The editors replied: *"Little Basis-- Rare instances have occurred where rocker arm has gone flying through valve cover, but incidence is so slight as to be statistically insignificant. Typical slur sure to be fostered by competitive dealers."*

In a technical report on the 1956 Chevrolet in *Motor Life*, mention was made of the 1955 rocker arm problem, explaining that it had been resolved. "It may well be, however, that the rpm limit will be held down due to the fact that all 1956 engines are equipped with hydraulic valve lifters. This is opposed to the 1955 practice in which

MOTOR TREND PERFORMANCE COMPARISONS FOR 1955

1955 Chev 6 Two-Ten w/OD 4-dr sedan 123hp @3800 rpm 235.5 cid MT 8/55	*1955 Chev V8 Two-Ten w/PG* 4-dr sedan 162 hp @4400 rpm 265 cid MT 1/55	*1955 Ford V-8 Customline* w/Fordomatic 4-dr sedan @4400 rpm 272 cid MT 1/55	*1955 Plymouth Belvedere V-8* w/PowerFlite 4-dr sedan 167hp @4400 rpm 260 cid MT 2/55

Top Speed

(In miles per hour over surveyed ¼ mile)

	Chev 6	Chev V8	Ford V-8	Plymouth
Fastest 1-way run	96.9	97.8	95.9	98.9
Slowest 1-way run	95.1	96.3	94.8	97.8
Average of 4 runs	95.7	97.3	95.2 (Average of four runs)	98.4 (Average of four runs)

Acceleration

(In seconds; checked with 5th wheel and electric speedometer)

Standing start

	Chev 6	Chev V8	Ford V-8	Plymouth
¼-mile	(70 mph) 19.9	(71 mph) 19.0	(74 mph) 19.4	(69.5 mph) 20.3
0–30 mph	4.7	4.3	4.5	5.4
0–60 mph	15.3	12.3	14.5	13.2
10–30 mph	4.1	3.1	3.3	4.2
30–50 mph	7.2	4.4	5.7	5.5
50–80 mph	17.7	15.5	19.8	16.2

Fuel Consumption

	Chev 6	Chev V8	Ford V-8	Plymouth
Steady 30 mph	32.5	20.6	18.5	18.7
Steady 45 mph	28.4	19.2	17.4	17.1
Steady 60 mph	21.9	15.8	14.0	15.2
Steady 75 mph	17.4		10.9	13.0
Stop-and-go driving over measured course	18.5	13.7	11.9	12.8
Tank average for (miles)	1608 miles 19.3	1241 miles 14.5	1386.1 miles 13.4	1134.6 miles 15.0

Stopping Distance

(To the nearest foot; checked with electrically actuated detonator.)

	Chev 6	Chev V8	Ford V-8	Plymouth
30 mph	33	33	33	30
45 mph	82	82	82	81
60 mph	146	146	178	173

the standard shift models were set up with solid tappets. This led to a very discouraging series of rocker stud replacements due to exuberant over-revving. The Powerglide models had the hydraulic lifters and, even in power kit form, were not subject to such failures. It wasn't that the PG owners were less enthusiastic but merely that the upper rev limit imposed by the pump-up speed of the lifters was around 5800 rpm. At speeds allowed by the solid tappets. the rocker studs popped out like champagne corks at a Polish wedding."

Chevrolet Service News, November, 1955, stated, "As a mid-season change in 1955, all V-8 engines were converted to hydraulic valve lifters. Since this same feature has been added to six-cylinder engines for the coming year, the need for periodic valve train adjustments to compensate for normal wear is now eliminated on all Chevrolet engines."

So it did happen, and some 22 years later, it surfaced again in an interview with Clare MacKichan: "I remember that rocker situation very well because I had one of the first ones built with the stamped rocker, and my wife was having a baby at the time, about three in the morning. I was on my way to the hospital and I had about ten miles and I was going rather rapidly and all of a sudden all hell broke loose and it was one of the rockers that cut loose..."

More than anything else, though, a major problem for Chevrolet Division was that V-8 production couldn't keep up with the dealer demand. It was not uncommon for customers to have to wait for the V-8 powered cars. During this time lapse they sometimes decided to purchase one of the other of the "low-priced three," and the sale was lost forever.

The startling performance of Chevy's new V-8 inevitably led to donning racing colors and chasing after the checkered flag. It started off quietly enough. In February, 1955, running the Daytona Beach "road and beach course" with

Chevrolet began pushing its NASCAR record almost as soon as the successes were achieved, and the ads packed a healthy punch...

CHEVROLET'S TAKING COMPETITION TO THE CLEANERS!

The records prove that in NASCAR Short Track events, '55 Chevrolets have rolled up almost twice as many points as their nearest competitor —really cooling the hot high-priced jobs and clobbering *everything* in their own price class.

Why?

Because the '55 Chevrolet V8 is a lot more than just a plain passenger car! There's real *sports car* handling in the accuracy of its Ball-Race steering, the broad base of its outrigger rear springs, the road grip of its spherical-joint front suspension. These things mean more fun for you behind the wheel—*and safer, surer control wherever you*

drive. You pass, stop, steer and take the turns with new confidence and security.

Look at it from any angle and the 1955 Chevrolet V8 is a lot more car than the low-price field has ever known before. It's easy to see why the 180-horsepower "Super Turbo-Fire"* version (with four-barrel carburetor, big manifold and dual exhausts) is setting the drag strips on fire.

And when you consider the *potential* in that ultra-light, ultra-compact powerplant—well, borrow one from your Chevrolet dealer and we won't have to do any more talking: *this* V8 can speak for itself!

Optional at extra cost.

 CHEVROLET DIVISION OF GENERAL MOTORS, DETROIT 2, MICHIGAN

CHEVROLET WINS AT ATLANTA!

THE NEW WINNER IN STOCK CAR COMPETITION

Chevrolet wins first and second place for another great victory! This official 50-mile NASCAR® competition at Atlanta, Ga. is a rugged test of acceleration, roadability and handling qualities. Here, again, Chevrolet beat all comers—including many of America's highest priced cars. This record-breaking performance is helping Chevrolet dealers win new prospects and buyers every month!

'National Association for Stock Car Auto Racing

New Products, New Progress CHEVROLET **for a new era of leadership**

More racing-based ads. Above, a word to the competition...

And a big, blasty announcement of Chevy's 1-2 Atlanta finish.

Chrysler 300s, Buicks and Oldsmobiles, Jack Radtke's Chevy V-8 finished a respectable tenth. In its own class, Chevrolet captured the four top positions, and eight out of the first 11 spots in the standing-start acceleration tests over a measured mile. In the straightaway running, open to cars delivered in Florida for $2500 or less, Chevrolets were first and second, and held seven of the first 11 places. Finally, in the two-way measured mile for cars of 250 to 299 cubic inches displacement, Chevrolet took three of the first five positions. By this time people were less apt to question what Chevrolet meant by "The Hot One."

As if its first performance wasn't enough, the Chevy V-8 ran to glory at the first NASCAR "short-track" race at Fayetteville, North Carolina. "Smokey Yunick had been preparing winning Hudsons for Herb Thomas in Grand National," writes Paul Van Valkenburgh*, but for the tighter tracks he built the Chevrolet, and Thomas won the first time out in it. Two weeks later Smokey tried it against the G.N. cars again at Columbia, S.C., and this time Fonty Flock won, beating his brother in one of the Chryslers. The next day at Hillsboro, N.C., Fonty was fifth, while Herb Thomas went out with a broken wheel.

"The new Chevrolet was a sensation, its performance was news as far north as Detroit, where people at Chevrolet Engineering and Chevrolet's ad agency, Campbell-Ewald, were getting ideas. Barney Clark and Jim Wangers jumped on the promotion possibilities immediately, and by June, they had Chevrolet NASCAR success advertised in both *Motor Trend* and the trade journal *Automotive News*."

Campbell-Ewald's message was blunt and to the point: "Who's Running Number ONE in competition where 'claims' don't count?" their ad rhetorically asked. "CHEVROLET--That's who! In NASCAR Short Track Division events, this '55 Chevrolet has brought home more winning points than any car in any price class. Engine and perform-

* Mr. Van Valkenburgh's comments above, and on page 148, are from his book, "Chevrolet-Racing ???", distributed by E.P. Dutton Co., 2 Park Avenue, New York, New York 10016.

ance *claims* (the allusion here was certainly to Chrysler's 300) don't count in this league. Here you've either got it or you haven't!"

Ed Cole, never very far from the scene of any action, observed the Chevrolet conquests thoughtfully. Soon he sent engineer Mauri Rose down to NASCAR country to investigate; Rose reported considerable potential in factory sponsorship of Smokey Yunick and other Chevrolet drivers. Rose himself took charge of engineering, with Yunick and Herb Thomas driving the cars, Smokey being responsible for race preparation. Chevrolet began putting heavy-duty and "export" parts into production--the same formula that had stood Hudson in such good stead for the previous four years. Thanks to its heads-up advertising agency, Chevy had gleaned much favorable publicity, and Rose was heading up a growing performance parts business.

"Chevrolet wasn't building race cars," Van Valkenburgh continues, "they were building production sedans that were suitable for racing...with the proper optional heavy-duty parts. As the racers broke components--wheels, axles, steering arms, spindles, etc.--Chevrolet produced heavier ones and made them available to everyone. That doesn't mean that everyone had to *buy* them though. Advertising was paying the racing bill, and if it looked like a certain driver could win, and he looked good in photographs, he might be able to get all the pieces and a car and put them on, for no more than his signature on a release. However, it wasn't an organized racing team. Everything passed through Yunick's shop, but everyone campaigned his own car."

The Chevrolet performance peaked at Darlington, South Carolina on Labor Day 1955: the Southern 500. Chevrolet was out for business, with 24 entries in the field of 69, and though there was stiff competition from Joe Weatherly and Curtis Turner in Fords, the Chevrolets "ate 'em up."

Herb Thomas taking first place in Southern 500, Darlington, South Carolina, Labor Day, 1955.

Herb Thomas alone on victory lap in Number 92.

Herb Thomas was first, at a 92.281 mph average, followed by Jim Reed in a Chevy, Tim Flock was third in a Chrysler 300, but Chevies additionally were fourth, seventh, eighth, ninth and tenth. Seven out of the first ten places: not a bad day's work!

These cars were rated at 195 horsepower (regular "Power-pack" plus Corvette camshaft and valve springs), and as reported by *Motor Trend*, had "a wide range of rear axles. They can use standard Chevy, Chevy trucks, and, conveniently enough, catalog-listed Oldsmobile variations. Both Thomas and Reed used 9.3 axles...Suspension changes on the cars (double shocks, Air-Lifts, general beefing-up, etc.) are permitted" by NASCAR. Modifications of engine and drive train were also allowed, with parts listed in factory manuals.

DARLINGTON DATA

1. Herb Thomas — Chevrolet
2. Jim Reed — Chevrolet
3. Tim Flock — Chrysler
4. Gwen Staley — Chevrolet
5. Larry Flynn — Ford
6. Buck Baker — Buick
7. Jake Maness — Chevrolet
8. Cotton Owens — Chevrolet
9. Bill Widenhouse — Chevrolet
10. Jim Massey — Chevrolet
11. Banks Simpson — Buick
12. Joe Eubanks — Oldsmobile
13. Marvin Panch — Chevrolet
14. Nace Mattingly — Ford
15. Jim Lewallen — Oldsmobile
16. Ralph Liguori — Mercury
17. Banjo Matthews — Oldsmobile
18. Dave Terrell — Oldsmobile
19. Bud Graham — Chevrolet
20. Bill Champion — Buick

And that wasn't the end of it. In October at Charlotte, North Carolina, Chevys again came home with the bacon, garnering 1-2-4-7-8-9-10 positions. Meanwhile, Marshall Teague was leading the AAA circuit with a Chevrolet. It was a good year for the "Hot One"--unquestionably.

And how did Chevrolet make out in the other race for the year, the one referred to in 1954 as **THE GREAT RACE**--the production battle with Ford Division? Competition was just as hearty there as it was on the track, with Ford extremely close as year end figures were tabulated. Plymouth, too, was becoming more than a distant runner with its production almost doubled, jumping from 400,000 in '54 to 743,000 in '55, because of its new styling, new V-8 engine, and emphasis on its sales program. But Ford was the big competitor.

Across the board pricing of the three was very comparative. Model availability was competitive, as well as choice of engines: Plymouth's new V-8 offered horsepower ranging from 157 to 177, Ford's V-8 from 162 to 182 hp, and Chevy's from 162 to 180 hp. The three corporations were expanding in mid-1955: Chrysler to the tune of $625 million, Ford by $625 million, and GM by $500 million. When the 1955 figures were all totaled what were the final production statistics between Ford and Chevrolet?

Ford had built 1,764,524 cars for 22.22 percent of the market. Chevrolet had built 1,830,038 or 23.04 percent of the market. It had been a nip-and-tuck year, but Chevy had come out on top by 65,514 units or a mere .82 percent of total production lead over Ford. But this bettered Chevy's lead in 1954, when it led by only 19,603 units, or a .36 percent of total production. The Great Race had

UNITED STATES PASSENGER CAR PRODUCTION
BY MONTH, CALENDAR 1954 AND 1955

1954	Jan.	Feb.	Mar.	Apr.	May	June	July	Aug.	Sept.	Oct.	Nov.	Dec.	Total
Chev.	117,025	110,593	131,151	140,588	130,956	130,456	122,120	133,158	37,690	72,440	131,615	156,573	1,414,365
Ford	118,677	115,995	134,948	128,190	125,698	126,541	115,549	120,378	114,143	30,420	115,660	148,563	1,394,762
Ply.	36,154	24,380	39,039	39,423	33,697	43,705	32,600	11,572	1,861	14,868	49,704	72,897	399,900

1955													
Chev.	154,517	153,494	173,030	163,176	164,055	130,668	172,020	164,011	130,533	85,171	181,519	157,844	1,830,038
Ford	143,761	137,175	157,672	153,940	153,294	149,105	143,891	140,454	106,083	162,597	163,245	153,308	1,764,524
Ply.	64,046	68,068	79,680	76,443	68,143	65,810	55,477	57,820	4,224	60,089	75,060	68,131	742,991

*Wards 1956 p. 37

been won by Chevrolet--again. This time it wasn't con-
tested with any R.L. Polk & Company "secondary analysis" figures. It was clean cut.

It seems almost ludicrous, looking back at *Fortune's*
words with regard to the automotive industry, in March
1955: "Sales projections for the current year are quite optimistic. They range from 5,500,000 cars...to 5,800,000
(plus 200,000 for export) predicted by GM's Harlow Curtice...At the moment a 5,800,000 year seems possible, but
not probable..." Nobody was capable of predicting 1955,
not *Fortune*, not even Curtice. It ended a full 40 percent
over *Fortune's* estimate: 7,942,131, 44 percent above

1954 production, 18 percent above previous record year
1950. *Almost eight million cars!*

It was a good year...1955. It was a good year for the in-
dustry--but especially good for Chevrolet. In his interview
with this writer, Clare MacKichan summed it up: "What
we were trying to do was change our whole image to the
public: from the older man's car to youth. And the car
was made to do it...the engine was made to do it...and we
did it."

But that wasn't the end of the story of these remarkable
Chevrolets. That V-8 engine had a lot of lung capacity left
--and Chevy's fine styling had a few more years to run, too.

Chevrolet's frontal appearance for 1956 bespoke the wider, lower and longer trend of mid-Fifties styling in this graceful manner.

CHAPTER THREE

1956: The Hot One's Even Hotter

Nineteen fifty-six: U.S. prosperity continued, but tension with Russia mounted. John Foster Dulles spoke of "the necessary art" of our Cold War position: "The ability to get to the verge without getting into the war." At home, North and South faced off again, with violent reaction in Dixie to the Supreme Court ruling against public school segregation. Still, Americans could turn away from internal and external problems, and become caught up in the colorful quadrennial tradition of national conventions. In due course, Dwight D. Eisenhower was re-elected, by an even larger margin than in 1952.

Motion picture fans gasped at the budgets of current epics. "War and Peace" was budgeted for a cool $6½ million. "The Ten Commandments" absorbed $13½ million. On the TV screen, the swiveling pelvis of irresistible Elvis appeared ofttimes below the eyes of the camera on The Ed Sullivan Show, and for several weeks, Presley's "Hound Dog," "Don't Be Cruel" and "I Want You, I Need You, I Love You" held down first, second and fifth place in platter sales.

In sports, we followed the New York Yankees as they turned back the Brooklyn Dodgers, four games to three, in the World Series, during which a righthander named Don Larsen pitched New York to the first perfect game--27 men up, 27 men down--in World Series history. November saw 21-year-old Floyd Patterson knock out Archie Moore, capturing the heavyweight title vacated by retiring Rocky Marciano. The next day, Army and Navy settled for a 7-7 tie in their 57th annual classic in Philadelphia.

All in all, it was a pretty good, typical Fabulous Fifties year, except in certain isolated areas like Archie Moore's house. For the auto industry, *Ward's* said 1956 added up to "a period of momentous change and adjustment...the only measure in which it appeared logy was in comparison to 1955...Unfortunately, before 1956 even started, prognosticators optimistically appraised it as the second-best year of all time"--they'd predicted 7.5 to eight million cars and trucks. And therein lay the rub: 1955 would be a tough act to follow.

Statistically 1956 looked pretty dismal. New car registrations, compared to 1955, were down 16.9 percent, from 7.1 million to 5.9 million, and car production was down 27 percent, from 7,942,131 to 5,801,864. Even though factory sales were the fourth highest in history, the three years that were higher were much too recent: 1950, 1953, 1955. At retail level the problem was magnified by excessive inventories built up by overly optimistic dealers--by the last of February there was a 43-day supply of cars, almost twice what it had been a year before.

The staggering independents only staggered more. Said Tom McCahill: "Studebaker-Packard, gasping like a wounded bass, was absorbed by Curtiss-Wright. American Motors was still finding the Rambler its only statistic worth noting. Unlike the immediate postwar years when you could have sold a motorized garbage can, competition 'firmed up' as they say on Madison Avenue." For a large number of dealers, most of them independents, the only healing agent would be time.

But for the main subject of these pages, 1956 was not all doom and gloom. Together with Ford and Rambler, Chevrolet enjoyed an increased sales penetration of low-priced cars--nearly 61 percent of the market against 57 percent in 1955. Chevrolet's January market was up 20,000 from the previous one, a statistic that caused particular cheering when it was found that Ford sales had declined 20,000 that same month...

Among a myriad of factors responsible for the 1956 "leveling process," one can perhaps single out loose credit as a major culprit. According to *Fortune*, "automobile paper outstanding has risen from $455 million at the end of 1945 to $3.1 billion at the end of 1948 to no less than $14.3 billion at the end of 1955 (over 360 percent since 1948). The proportion of cars bought on time has risen from 40 percent to more than 70 percent. Cars alone accounted for nearly $4 billion of 1955's $6-billion rise in consumer credit." The industry had offered some unusual-

ly attractive cars in 1955, and peddled an enormous amount of them through relaxed credit terms, in effect borrowing from future (1956) sales.

A high volume manufacturer like Chevrolet was in a better position to withstand these sad portents than smaller volume competitors, and in fact, Chevy did particularly well by comparison. Dropping by about 200,000 units, it still managed to produce 88 percent of its 1955 volume. Ford, for example, could only score 77 percent, Buick 68, Plymouth 60. Down in the cellar league, a troubled Packard saw only 13,000-odd sales in 1956, against close to 70,000 the year before, resulting in a frightening 18 percent of its 1955 production. American Motors, which had plummeted from 160,000 to about 104,000, was down to 64 percent. The only makes to largely escape statistical doldrums were Lincoln (which actually increased production 17 percent, thanks to total restyling rather than to the disappointingly scarce Mark II Continental), Cadillac (a shade down but not much) and Imperial (about the same).

Although 1956 was not generally an "all new" year stylewise, many innovations did occur in design and engineering that generally improved the product. Automatic transmissions were more common than ever before, being fitted to three-quarters of new car production--with Chrysler's pushbutton PowerFlite scoring close to 80 percent on Chrysler cars. Low-priced automobiles like Chevrolet were the key to automatic's improved status, since the higher-priced cars had been powered by V-8s, and shifted automatically, for a longer period.

Power accessories and two-tone paint jobs enjoyed rising popularity. Safety, too, was emphasized, loudly by Ford, more quietly by GM and Studebaker-Packard, though there is little evidence that safety features greatly enhanced salability.

For General Motors, 1956 started off with a traditional blast: the Motorama. It opened at the Waldorf on January

Oldsmobile Division's 1956 Motorama star was the exotic, fast-looking Golden Rocket, with automatic lift-up roof sections fitted.

Pontiac's 1956 Club de Mer boasted 300 horsepower.   Buick's dark metallic red Centurion wowed crowds.   Eldo Brougham Town Car presaged production.

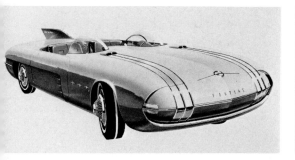

The softly rounded lines of Chevrolet Division's 1956 show car, the Impala, were more suggestive of 1958 production than 1957.

19th, and well over two million people had attended before it closed in Boston at the end of April. Traveling to Miami, Los Angeles, and San Francisco as in 1955, the Motorama displayed some spectacular machines. Pontiac's Firebird II, "a futuristic car crammed with advanced engineering ideas," was powered by a gas turbine engine; its "Club de Mer," a three-foot-high Cerulean blue finned affair, was nevertheless capable of comfortably housing Harley Earl's six-and-a-third feet. Oldsmobile displayed the 275 horsepower "Golden Rocket," a striking gold two-seater with automatically raising roof panels, and Buick's four-passenger "Centurion" had an all-glass bubble top, a swiveling steering column for left- or right-hand drive, and a television screen instead of a mirror for keeping tabs on following traffic. Cadillac's star was the "Eldorado

Brougham Town Car," said to be aimed "at the youthful wealthy," with an open chauffeur's compartment as per town car tradition.

Chevrolet's Motorama entry was the "Impala," a name we'd be hearing more of in the future, strictly experimental for 1956, but displaying many innovative safety features: a padded bar across the instrument panel, a padded steering wheel, low and graceful styling. "Long before the Motorama of 1956 is broken up," said *Colliers*, "the GM team will gather around in Harlow Curtice's office, look at one another and say, 'What the hell are we going to do next year?'"

It wasn't hard for the ad agency to come up with a sales slogan for Chevrolet in 1956. Chevy's impressive performance at the Southern 500, its sprint up Pikes Peak, its

1955 supremacy in NASCAR short track racing made it easy. The word was out as the '56s debuted at the end of October: "The Hot One's Even Hotter." And it wasn't all meaningless chatter. In September 1955, driving a 1956 Bel Air sport sedan with 205 hp Super Turbo-Fire V-8, Zora Arkus-Duntov charged up Pikes Peak in 17 minutes, 24.05 seconds, establishing a new American stock sedan record for the 12.5-mile ascent, fully two minutes better than the previous best time.

There wasn't any doubt by now that performance was Chevy's middle name. Tom McCahill, for example, voted it

Attention-grabbing advertisements were '56 forte.

Zora Arkus-Duntov sparked Chevy's performance cars.

the "best performance buy in the world." After testing the '56, he allowed as how "it would whiz by a Duesenberg like Halley's Comet and the vacuum as it went by would suck the stork off a Hispano-Suiza." *Motor Life*, a shade more conservative, said the 1956 model was much hotter than the '55, which had been pretty outstanding itself.

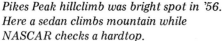

Pikes Peak hillclimb was bright spot in '56.
Here a sedan climbs mountain while
NASCAR checks a hardtop.

Even staid old *Consumer Reports* admitted that "the Chevvy [sic] is as quick and sure-footed as a cat." Sports car-oriented *Road & Track*, already amazed by the 1955's performance, agreed that Chevrolet was even hotter in 1956 thanks to a 14 percent increase in horsepower and improved handling.

But the thing that sales prospects saw first, then, now and always, was styling--and GM attempted to make the new Chevrolet as visually different as possible within the context of mild facelifting. It was expensive alteration: the corporation poured some $40 million into body redesign, a million dollars alone focused on giving the fenders what was called "the Cadillac flat look." In general, the body was bulked up, but careful attention was paid to insure that it didn't *look* heavy, and that its basic simplicity of line was preserved.

In *Fortune*, interviews with Chevy and Ford dealers summarized the differences for 1956 between the two fierce rivals. Said a Chevy dealer, "We got better in 1956, they stayed where they were." A Ford man replied that "Chevrolet made more of a change in '56 than Ford did. Ford didn't give the public a different enough car. A guy driving a '55 Ford didn't see any point in trading it in for a '56." Chevrolet's former stigma of being "an old man's car" had been so completely turned about that it was forgotten. Said another Chevy dealer, "We've had more kids, screwballs and race fans in here this year than we ever thought was possible. Sometimes we wish they'd stayed with Ford, but they buy cars, too."

The front end received the most radical change with the replacement of the Earl-inspired "Ferrari grille." Chevrolet now went to a more contemporary--and acceptable--

massive latticework, spanning the full width of the car and incorporating large rectangular parking lights. Possibly, Styling Staff had been listening when Floyd Clymer's 1955 report had the egg-crate grille down as a leading no-no; GM was always quick to grasp the public mood.

Interestingly, *Motor Trend* had maintained that Chevrolet was happy with the '55 grille. Replying to a reader question as to whether a crash-program existed to change it for 1956, *MT* had this to say: "Altho' competitive stylists say that not enough attention was given to proper angling of chrome for glint and glitter, Chevy management is proud of their lithe, Ferrari-like design. They are selling like hot cakes [the grille wasn't the reason] and will set Chevy style pattern for at least another year. This widespread rumor was started by envious competition of the all new car." *Motor Trend*, not for the first time, couldn't have been more wrong. In the magazine's defense, its information probably came from the stylists rather than the marketing department.

Clare MacKichan discussed this abrupt grille change in some detail with the author: "We had two cars out at the proving grounds with different grilles for the '55 program, Harley Earl's narrow Ferrari-inspired design, and a wider one. At that time it was chosen to go to the narrow one for 1955." Just how unpopular was the '55 egg crate, and was that why it didn't last? Yes, MacKichan said, "this wider '56 grille design was the result of people not accepting the narrow grille. We *were* going to continue with the narrow grille for a period of time, on that '56 Chevy, but a different design and different pattern. Then we had a lot of pressure from Chevrolet [sales], so we did this alternate grille which appeared on the 1956 car, almost exactly as it had been sketched."

The new grille was integral with generally revised frontal styling. Above, a new, flatter hood extended four inches

The '55 grille theme was suggested slightly in '56.

farther forward before dropping to meet the grille, modifying the snub-nosed appearance of the 1955 model. "The new flatter hood," said brochures, "further exemplifies the low, wide, rectangular new front end treatment." The final touch was a vee'd effect, carried out on hood, grille, bumper and accessory bumper chrome. A new hood ornament was devised, and below that was mounted a large Chevrolet emblem on sixes, or a smaller emblem over a wide chrome "V" on V-8s. The emblems were repeated respectively on rear decks. Headlight hoods were restyled, and the costly fender modification resulted in higher and straighter lines from the cowl forward. One might refer to it as "the million dollar look," because that's about what it cost Chevrolet.

At the sides, the 1956 Chevy was further removed from its predecessor. Trim moldings and two-toning dictated new front and rear wheel openings, gracefully flared and elongated, giving an overall fleet, rakish, swept-back appearance. The two-toning was a major departure from 1955 concepts. Said Clare MacKichan, "I remember on the '56 we tried a lot of different kinds of two-toning, and this led us into a really different way. Everything was to make it look lower, wider and longer, especially on the Two-Ten and Bel Air. This kind of two-tone treatment on the side... the flared wheel openings...they all helped to do it." Carl Renner looks back on the 1956 facelift with pleasure: "I

A popular 1956 feature was the hidden fuel filler cap.

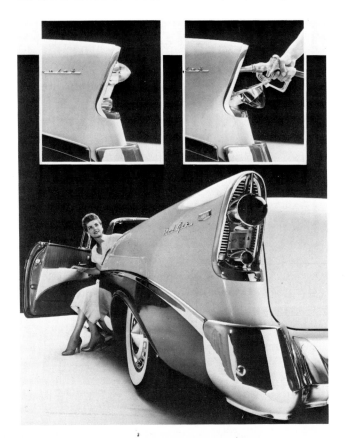

like the '56 side treatment. It is not as heavy as the '57. It has a lot of zip--visual zip."

But it's impossible not to conclude that the 1956 Chevrolet was a lot busier than the 1955, and this characteristic was particularly stressed at the rear. The simple, neat taillamp treatment of '55 was replaced by a complicated design incorporating taillight, brake light and backup light in a chrome plated pot metal sculpture. The left unit contained the fuel filler, hinged and concealed à la Cadillac. Carl Renner views the alteration as "more or less an advance, next step in design from the '55--exaggerated, elongated, [with] a little more schmaltz." Were the stylists prepared to admit what so many insist, that "facelifts" generally complicate a clean original design? Yes, if Clare MacKichan is any authority: "I really think the '55 was right, and as we went along [it became] a little less so. When you have to take the same body shell and change it, you have to apply things. Nineteen fifty-five was the pure statement. From a designer's viewpoint certainly, the '55 is the superior car."

MacKichan's retrospect is reinforced somewhat by a development of the times. J.C. Whitney & Co., paragon of customizers the world over, soon began to offer smooth plastic taillights that completely covered the stock 1956 units, rendering them more on the order of the clean original.

All of the preceding stated, one should be careful to note the relative refinement of Chevy's approach to 1956 restyling. Remember that 1956 was a notoriously memorable year for rear end alterations. The reader may recall the "tacked on" fins of the Studebaker Golden Hawk, which made a good original design somehow less effective; or the chrome bolt-on fins of the Dodge Custom Royal Lancer; or the even sillier uplifted posterior of the 1956 Plymouth. One reporter, summarizing cars like the latter, said "they end in aquiline beaks that sniff disdainfully off

The 1956 Plymouth's fins were obviously added late...

So were the 1956 Dodge's, which were even taller.

into space, like ships' figureheads in reverse." By comparison, Chevrolet was being modest.

The 1956 line was again offered in One-Fifty, Two-Ten and Bel Air models, with a total of 19 different body styles and 11 power teams, dressed in ten solid colors or 14 two-tones dependent on series and body style. The even hotter hot one featured "increased horsepower and bold new Motoramic styling," with a four-door sport sedan (hardtop) in the Two-Ten and Bel Air series advertised as "embodying the youthful lines of a convertible, the practicality of a hardtop, and the convenience of a four-door sedan." Growing public interest in station wagons also caused Chevrolet to offer six different kinds in 1956, by adding a new four-door nine-passenger Two-Ten Beauville, and enlarging its Bel Air Beauville wagon from six- to nine-passengers. The rest of the 1956 range remained the same as in 1955.

The four-door hardtop had its origins with the Cadillac Orleans show car of 1953, and was pioneered by General Motors in the form of Oldsmobiles and Buicks during 1955. But the Orleans, Clare MacKichan points out, wasn't the

direct connection. In reality the four-door hardtop "just sort of evolved out of the two-door hardtop, out of production, the same as wrap-around windshields."

This model's body engineering was explained in *Chevrolet Service News*: "Each rear door is mounted on a pillar extending upward from the floor to the beltline. To add the necessary rigidity, the pillar is heavily reinforced and welded to the floor through wide flared joints at its base. Further body stability is added by a repositioned and re-shaped body cross member which extends across the frame between the two rear door pillars."

Although width and height remained the same, 1956 Chevrolets were longer by two inches (coupes and sedans) or three inches (wagons). The new length and side treatment gave the '56 a much longer look. Inside, the same basic dashboard was retained, but the Bel Air's "bow tie" dash of 1955 was abandoned in favor of rectangular slots. The author asked MacKichan why this change occurred. "You get a whole generation of 'bow ties' and you've had enough," he replied. "It was sort of like the Pontiac Indian--we had them on everything." The appliqués came

In contrast to most of its opposition, the 1956 Chevrolet's styling came off as a very well-planned, well-executed, modest facelift.

from the Harrington & King company, which made perforated metal for GM. The slots of the 1956 version, Chevy said, used "an elongated rectangular grille pattern similar to that of the radiator grille." With the exception of different knobs, this was the sole change to dashboard design for 1956.

Restyled interior and exterior trim differed in the three series, as it had in 1955, and any power team was available with any body style. The One-Fifty series included the same four body types: two- and four-door sedans, a two-door utility sedan, and a two-door six-passenger Handyman station wagon. Sedan deliveries, though not part of

Chevy advertising pushed hard for fleet/cab sales.

The 1956 Two-Ten sport coupe was Chevrolet's economy hardtop.

The 1956 Two-Ten four-door sedan was often sold two-toned.

the passenger car line, could be had with One-Fifty trim.

A special effort was made to rid the One-Fifty line of its austere look, to aim it away from the fleet sales category and toward the individual buyer. One-Fifty interiors received gold vinyl trim on bolsters and side panels, harmonizing with gold-flecked upholstery. On the outside, One-Fifties wore side trim for the first time in the history of the model, enabling them to use   two-tone paint jobs.   A

stainless steel molding ran from near the headlights back along two-thirds of the car length, where it joined a sash molding of simulated vent slots which originated at the beltline dip, reaching downward and forward to meet it. Bright metal reveal moldings covered the rubber windshield and rear window surrounds. The package was successful: though model year production was 209,000 less in 1956, 20,000 more One-Fifties were sold.

New in 1956 was Bel Air nine-passenger wagon with third seat.

Bel Air sport coupe interior followed the established theme.

Two-Ten models were now available in eight body styles: two- and four-door sedan, Delray club coupe, two-door sport coupe, four-door sport sedan, and three station wagons--a two-door Handyman and four-door Townsman (both six-passenger), and four-door, nine-passenger Beauville. Two-Ten interiors featured patterned cloth: "horizontal ribs separated by silver threads and a dash pattern which is a darker tone than the basic cloth color." This combined with "textured vinyl with a frosted metallic dust appearance" for the bolsters and facings. The Delray club coupe was restyled with an attractive all-vinyl interior not unlike 1955's. On the outside, the Two-Ten horizontal molding extended rearward to the bumper in a gently descending arc; the sash molding ran downward from the dip in the beltline to meet it, as on the One-Fifty. For two-toned models, an additional small molding ran from the side bar to the top of the front fender, serving as a paint divider.

The top-of-the-line 1956 Bel Air was available in seven different styles: two- and four-door sedans, a sport coupe and sport sedan, a convertible and two wagons including the Nomad and Beauville. Bel Airs featured luxurious Jacquard weave nylon-faced cloth on seats and backrests, combined with a triangular motif leather-grained vinyl set off by a plastic-covered silver button in the "V" of each seat back. Thick carpeting front and rear completed the package. Outside, the newness really showed: the full-length, downward sloping side molding of the Two-Ten was accompanied by a second molding that formed a "comet trail effect further highlighted on two-tone models by running the generally lighter roof and rear deck color forward through the side and door panels onto the front fenders." The Bel Air nameplate and small crest were mounted on the rear fenders forward of the taillights. (One-Fifties and Two-Tens carried "Chevrolet" script here.)

As MacKichan informed the writer, two-toning led "into

a really different way" of styling cars. For Chevy, it was the first time more than a rear fender, trunk or roof treatment was involved. Two-toning was a trend, of course, and like the fin business it sometimes went too far. DeSoto and Packard had even dared market three-tone models, in their Fireflite Coronado and Caribbean of 1955, and soon half the industry had followed suit. There was a point at which all these colors, chrome and stainless steel seemed almost to appear at random, indicating that the designers--or at least the marketing people--were completely oblivious to genuine styling. In this area *Consumer Reports* was undoubtedly accurate when it described such effects as "a dismembered look...bearing much less relation to the car's basic lines, shape and function than do the colors on a zebra or giraffe." Chevrolet, thankfully, never became involved with three-toning and interestingly, neither did Ford or Plymouth. Apparently, this gauche method of styling automobiles was reserved only for high-priced bad taste. But for Chevrolet, the 1956 two-toning accomplished its goal: an obvious change from 1955, a visual modification that made the car look lower and longer in accord with Marketing's game plan for the middle Fifties. Relative to its contemporaries, the '56 may be set down in the upper middle end of the field: not quite as clean as, say, the 1956 Imperial, but a whole lot more timeless than the baroque Dodges, Studebakers and Packards and probably a better styling job than either Plymouth's or Ford's. And it still looks pretty good today.

One of the interesting developments of 1956 was the sudden transposition of the Ford and Chevy images. The arch rivals had for years gambled respectively on performance and "reliability," and many saw Chevrolets as dull, unimaginative four-wheeled transportation devices for what Tom McCahill called "old dowagers in Queen Mary hats." But in 1956, Ford had gone on its celebrated

A striking convertible by anybody's yardstick: 1956 Bel Air.

A definite look of speed and motion in the Bel Air hardtop.

A four-door station wagon from the 1956 Bel Air model line.

Undoubtedly the most stylish of the 1956 Ford-Chevy-Plymouth four-door hardtops was Chevrolet's sleek Bel Air sport sedan.

and disastrously unsuccessful safety kick, while Chevrolet, the "Hot One," was, as they said, Even Hotter. As one journalist summed it up, "Engine soup has more appeal than safety belts." But Chevrolet's claim was more than just puffery.

Never resting upon its laurels, the Division reached back into 42 years of valve-in-head engine experience to incorporate necessary improvements in both six and V-8. With the horsepower race in full swing, the "Blue Flame 140" six of 235.5 cubic inches replaced both the 123 and 136 hp engines of 1955, and could be coupled to standard, overdrive or Powerglide transmission. A new feature of this engine was a higher lift camshaft and hydraulic valve lifters, both furnished formerly only with the Powerglide

option. Other improvements included durable aldipped (aluminum coated) extra-allow exhaust valves. The 140's compression ratio was increased to 8:1 (from 7.5:1 in 1955), its torque being 210 at 4200 rpm.

The "Turbo-Fire V-8," still with 265 cubic inches, used the same camshaft with standard or overdrive transmission and developed 162 hp. With Powerglide-equipped models, a new higher-lift cam raised power to 170 hp at 4400 rpm, and torque to 257 pounds-feet at 4400 rpm. Optional was a "power-pack" consisting of higher-lift cam, and 9.25:1 compression cylinder head, four-barrel carburetor, special intake manifolds and dual exhausts pushing out 205 bhp at 4600 rpm. And an even more powerful unit was available with Corvette equipment, boosting horsepower to 225 at

5200 rpm. Cole's V-8 was beginning to stretch out--but there was more to come.

Additional features for 1956 V-8s included a full flow oil filter (evidently a mandatory option), full-pressure lubrication to the valve lifter gallery with metered pressure to the overhead mechanism. A new mounting for the generators reduced vibration and noise. To guard against water and foreign matter, the starter solenoid plunger was shielded by a neoprene boot, and another seal, of rubber, was placed between the cover and base of the voltage regulator. The exposed starter motor linkage was coated with lubriplate to prevent water accumulation, and the solenoid case was sealed. The wiring harness was split in two at the dashboard connection, to facilitate assembly and servicing. A shroud on the air cleaner made for quieter induction. All V-8 clutches used woven asbestos facing, and a high-capacity coil spring clutch replaced the diaphragm spring variety on Super Turbo-Fire models. Rear engine mounts were reformed for decreased noise and vibration, an electric water temperature gauge replaced the former tube type, enlarged exhaust crossover passages made for quicker cold weather warm-ups. Revising the tailpipe design and hangers permitted passage of a second pipe. Thus dual exhausts were now made available in station wagons and sedan deliveries when the Super Turbo-Fire was specified.

Suspension changes had also been made. The length of the front coil springs had been increased and the spring rate at each front wheel decreased from 109 to 100 pounds-per-inch. This resulted in less tendency to nose dive. Rear springs were improved by widening the hangers by an inch, thus allowing more rubber in the bushing to resist compression from axle side thrusts. Six-leaf rear springs, standard on the nine-passenger Beauville, were optional on other wagons.

It should not be assumed that Chevrolet left safety to Ford in 1956, despite the latter's widely touted program of life-saving improvements. Chevrolet *was* working on safety, just not making much noise about it. In July 1955 GM had added crash-proof door locks; these were carried over for 1956. The new Guide T-3 sealed beam headlamps featured three-point, quick-adjustment aiming, and they increased low-beam visibility to 80 feet. Seat belts became available as optional equipment. A padded instrument panel, consisting principally of fiberglass with a thin layer of cotton wadding beneath the vinyl exterior, not only protected passengers from sudden impact but reduced glare emanating from the painted dash.

Optional factory equipment included power steering ($92), power brakes ($38), power windows and front seats ($155). Factory air conditioning had been reduced to $430 from the towering $565 of 1955. A variety of minor accessories were added: a rear-mounted radio antenna (the '57s would sprout two of these). "Continental" spare tire kits (never as popular in their day as they are among collectors now) were among the goodies available at extra cost.

This was Chevrolet for 1956. Introduced in imaginative colors--Crocus yellow, Laurel green, Sierra gold, Adobe beige--the cars for spring appeared in a half dozen new shades--as Calypso cream and Grecian gold, and Inca silver and Imperial ivory, the latter in Lucite's new acrylic lacquers.

Chevrolet continued to enjoy a good press in 1956. Its styling, said Joe Wherry, was "the most restrained of all General Motors cars; it should have wide appeal with the new wider wrap-around grille. Evolutionary styling maintains [the] car's high resale value." The wider grille was completely successful, if Clymer's polls were any guide: owners surveyed ranked it the number one best-liked exterior styling feature--in 1955 it had been the number one complaint.

Imaginative photography and good-looking models were standard fare in 1956. Left, the optional lap-type safety belts. Above, electric window lifts. Right, alternate usage of the sparkling "Continental" rear tire mount on a 1956 Chevrolet Two-Ten four-door sedan.

There did arise some complaints about interior accommodations. *Motor Trend's* Jim Lodge criticized the limited rearward travel of the front seat, and like Wherry he noted that the rearview mirror "still was not wide enough to take full advantage of the broad expanse of rear glass," while admitting that a wider mirror would cause a blind spot. Clymer complained about weak springs in the front seat: "the small of my back sometimes hits the brace inside the seatback when going over rough bumps." Sport sedan headroom was considered somewhat restricted, and testers noted that the headliner was separated from the steel top by only a half-inch of padding. Another problem Wherry noticed was the headlamp dimmer switch, mounted "almost directly against the side panel and immediately below the louvered air vent. When one jabs the foot down on the dip switch to lower the headlight beams, the shoe is likely to scrape against this vent louver. Aside from possibly scraping the shoe, the sole can become trapped in the louvers and a sudden raising of the foot to switch to high beams becomes a clumsy operation."

Styling is not ordinarily related to handling, but *Motor Trend* had a telling observation vis-á-vis the '56 Chevies: "Styling--whether it means impressive bulges or is content with modest overhangs, fender upheavals, and the like--can have a definite effect on the pleasures of handling a car. The Chevy's restraint here makes it pleasanter to drive."

THE HOT ONE

A COLOR PORTFOLIO

S·1955

Stebbins

In a rendering for this book, designer Chuck Stebbins illustrates original planned 1955 trunk contour.

Right, the 1955 Bel Air sport coupe. Below, 1954 Motorama cars. From top, the Corvette, a non-production Corvette hardtop, Corvette Nomad and Corvair.

1956 Bel Air sport coupe.

The 1956 Bel Air Nomad.

The 1957 Bel Air sport coupe.

1957 Bel Air convertible.

The 1957 Bel Air Nomad.

Two other distinguishing features that helped Chevrolet win *MT*'s "best handling" award were its lightweight V-8 engine and excellent weight distribution, and its overall compact size--which *MT* felt was a definite advantage in battling express-type traffic.

The Chevrolet's size and handling were generally agreed to be among its best features. In Floyd Clymer's interviews, 48.5 percent of respondents listed handling as the "best-liked" feature, compared to only 30 percent in 1955's poll. *Consumer Reports* said Chevy took "a definite lead over its competitors, with its excellent cornering and top-notch road-holding...an exceptionally easy car to take over the road--even a winding road--at a good clip." And *Motor Life* said racing drivers agreed that Chevy handling was just as important to its oval track successes as its performance: "the relatively light engine and spherical-joint front suspension are big factors in Chevrolet's fine road-ability."

The 225 hp version was tried by Tom McCahill for *Mechanix Illustrated*. "In my opinion these cars, in order to stay together in hard use, definitely should have a stabilizer bar in the front end," Tom stated. "You can buy this as an accessory in nearly all Chevrolet dealers, but I think the factory should have tossed it in as standard. The front end has been beefed-up over '55--so has the whole car as a matter of fact--but it still needs the stabilizer bar. When I was testing this car...we hit a two-foot rut and the whole front end made a crashing noise similar to dropping an anvil on plate glass. If I hadn't braced myself...I'd have been riding the hood ornament bareback. A little more guts in the front end and this would be a much greater car." *Motor Trend*, on the other hand, thought flat-out handling pretty good. In Zora Duntov's 205 hp Pikes Peak car with Chevrolet engineer Mauri Rose at the wheel, Walt Woron and Don MacDonald cruised at speeds up to 80 mph. "We were

in a four-wheel drift practically all the time," they reported, "except when we switched from a left to a right-hand turn. At no time did the car want to break loose." Fine testimony, that.

Outstanding complaints about the mechanical package seemed to surround the brakes and the somewhat harder ride. *Consumer Reports* said the former tended toward "erratic operation, sometimes causing the car to pull to one side, sometimes to the other." *Motor Trend* felt Chevy brakes compared favorably to those of Ford and Plymouth, but in truth American drum brakes were no great shakes in 1956 and didn't start to really improve until the Sixties, when manufacturers began using special linings like sintered-metallic—introduced, by the way, by Chevrolet. Observers felt that the ride was a bit firm, but concluded that cushy ride had been "sacrificed on the altar

The '56 dash perforations were oblongs rather than bow-ties.

Sport sedan roof is welded to main body on the production line.

Ed Cole's potent V-8 meets mate at the engine drop during 1956.

Final metal finishing in '56; finish quality was held good.

A Two-Ten model four-door sedan at the body drop, early 1956.

ont end sheet metal, typical for most production lines in and out of GM, was sub-assembled first, then added to main body.

More 1956 advertising, reflecting the performance now being offered, and lifestyles in the Fabulous Fifties, starring Chevies.

of roadability." Said Jim Lodge, "It's good. Not on the soft side, Chevy ride benefits from car's inherent stability--that is, passengers aren't pitched or rocked from side to side on twisting roads, or see-sawed back and forth in stop-and-go driving. Seats aren't soft either, but they soak up a great deal of chassis movement, level out most minor disturbances. Washboard roads are felt throughout the body, aren't too objectionable on a seat-of-the-pants evaluation."

But the outstanding feature of the 1956 Chevy had to be its performance, and of this praise was high. *Motor Trend* awarded it the title, "best performance per dollar." *Motor Life*, *Road & Track* and *Mechanix Illustrated* all echoed these conclusions. "Where the new car should make its biggest showing, 50 to 80 mph--time was lowered 3.5 seconds from stock '55 time, 0.9 seconds from the '55 powerpack's 12.9 second time," said *ML*. "The new powerpack was noticeably livelier than last year's 180 hp job at turnpike speeds."

Motor Life tested two 1956 Chevys, with 170 and 205 hp. The difference between them was significant:

	170 hp	*205 hp*
0-30 mph (seconds)	4.1	3.2
0-60 mph (seconds)	11.9	8.9
50-80 mph (seconds)	15.1	9.2
top speed (mph)	98.2	108.7

Road & Track was almost dumbfounded with the improvement in performance of the 205 engine versus the 180 hp version it had tested the year before; its car exceeded 111 mph flat out. The top speed, the magazine said, "furnished a perfect opportunity for an object lesson on axle ratios:

rpm @ 111 mph	5700	5140	4940	3990
Ratio	4.11	3.70	3.55	2.88 (OD)

"Since the engine develops its peak bhp at 4600 rpm," *Road & Track* continued, "it is possible that the car might go still faster with the 3.55 axle which is standard equipment on the Powerglide models. However the 3.70 ratio is an excellent compromise as can be seen by comparing last year's acceleration times with those obtained on the 1956 test car."

	'55 180 hp *4.11 axle*	*'56 205 hp* *3.70 axle*	*time* *gain*
0-30 mph	2.9	3.0	------
0-40 mph	5.7	4.1	1.6
0-50 mph	7.2	6.8	0.4
0-60 mph	9.7	9.0	0.7
0-70 mph	13.1	11.1	2.0
0-80 mph	18.8	16.5	2.3
0-90 mph	28.0	21.8	6.2
standing ¼ mi.	17.4	16.6	0.8

"This table shows that the 14 percent increase in horsepower more than offsets the 10 percent reduction in axle ratio. It might also be noted that the improvement in 0 to 40 and 0 to 70 times are partially the result of higher speed shift points, for last year's test car had to shift from first gear at 34 to 37 mph and from second at 61 and 66 mph. Incidentally the 1956 car has hydraulic valve lifters, whereas the 1955 car did not. Nevertheless, valve bounce speed remains the same at about 5600 rpm!

"The 1956 powerpack gives only 3 percent more peak torque, but at 4600 rpm the torque is 234 foot-pounds [sic] as compared to only 205 foot-pounds in 1955. This is a gain of 14 percent and more importantly a drop of only 12.7 percent below the peak torque at 3000 rpm as compared to a drop of 21 percent in the 1955 model.

"Without a doubt the greatest charm of this car is its smooth, quiet running engine. Even though the compression ratio is extremely high (9.25 to 1) it was impossible to make it 'ping' on full throttle at any speed. Once or twice we detected a slight knock on part throttle at very low speed when lugging and on a cold (35° F.) start, after sitting all night, one of the hydraulic tappets 'tapped' for about 10 seconds. But, the surge of power (actually torque) is there at all times and knowing of the ultra-short stroke, one gets the impression that this engine would be impossible to 'blow-up' even under brutal treatment."

There was little, in fact, that *Road & Track* did *not* like about the 1956 Chevy. Mainly, its complaints were directed toward a minor detail, the three-speed column shift, a notorious product which continues to exist because it is

Ed Cole himself proves advantages of '56 engineering.

inexpensive, and those who order it generally don't mind. It was, *R&T* asserted, "surprisingly noisy on the indirect gears. And, like last year, we found the control linkage an absolute nuisance, even when making lazy shifts. It is noisy, sloppy and impossible to throw fast shifts without bending the control rods. The car starts off with a rush

even in second gear, but the enthusiast purchaser would be well advised to order the new Corvette 'stick-shift' controls and have them installed on the floor. Some people claim that all companies are neglecting their stick-shift cars to encourage sales of the automatic transmissions, which almost appears to be true, in this case."

It is worth mentioning the hand-stand reaction of Tom McCahill, to the aforementioned 225 hp engine, as the final testimony to 1956 Chevy performance: "Chevrolet has come up with a poor man's answer to a hot Ferrari...here's an engine that can wind up tighter than the E string on an East Laplander's mandolin...well beyond 6000 rpm without blowing up like a pigeon egg in a shotgun barrel."

McCahill knew of what he spoke. He had just directed the Daytona Speed Trials, having the unpleasant duty of disqualifying four of the front-running Chevys which "mysteriously" tossed their fan belts--one of them while passing the traps at 136 mph, turning close to 7000 rpm. Not wishing to go into the cause of why the belts came off, McCahill noted that the instant they did the engines would pick up as much as 15-25 hp. It seemed, *Time* noted later, "a quadruple coincidence" that four of Mauri Rose's fastest cars lost their belts in time to "make their runs without wasting the fraction of power used to turn radiator fans and generators."

Curious about this "tossing the fan belt" exposé, the author questioned Vince Piggins, now manager of Chevrolet Product Promotion, who threw some light on the problem. "That was just before I came to work for Chevrolet," Piggins says. "They had quite a time with those fan belts because the grooves weren't deep enough. Shortly after I began here there was a big program going on making new fan belt pulleys with deeper grooves just for that reason. Some additional technology came out on the belt composition and we ended up with the Goodyear Three T belt.

GM and Division brass celebrate Chevy's 35,000,000th, 1956.

"You get a standing wave in a belt with high rpm--and we got some high rpm on the beach at top speed--and that standing wave would just throw the belt right off. They weren't prepared down there at Daytona for any way to fix them. It just isn't something you can do overnight-- redesign the pulleys."

Later Unk had the opportunity to take one of these cars out--with its fan belt on: "We first ran it on the beach and then headed for some hardtop stuff for true accelera- tion times. When you jump the accelerator on one of these crickets, even on a glue surface, the wheels spin around like a Waring Blender and at the moment you make contact you shoot ahead--*zoom!* You blast up the road as if you had a barrel of nitro in the tail. Zero to 30 mph averages 3.2 seconds, zero to 60 mph 8.9 seconds and in 12 seconds, you're doing 70 mph. This is just about May, June and July faster than the Chevrolets of just two or three years ago."

And did they blow up? No way! "These engines de- pend on high rpm for their performance, 6200 and up. This would have most other American engines exploding if their valves hadn't started floating some 600 rpm earlier. Ed Cole, who designed this engine, deserves a world of credit. Realizing that he built it with a price factor and general usefulness in mind, Cole doesn't have to take a back seat to anyone at Mercedes, Ferrari or any of the other accepted automotive greats...ounce for ounce and cubic inch for cubic inch, this Chevrolet engine is the greatest performing engine ever built in America, bar none. Risking repetition and considering that low price was a major design factor, this engine might very well be rated the greatest competition engine ever built. It un- doubtedly is, from a dollar-and-cents standpoint...

"You old readers may remember that as long as eight or nine years ago we pointed out that if the American manu-

facturers ever decided to build the best-performing cars in the world they could do it in a matter of months. The fas- test high-performance sedan built in Europe today is the Bentley Continental, costing roughly $20,000. This Chev- rolet, costing ten percent of that, could eat it alive even with an unwarmed-up engine."

Not all of this was standard McCahill hyperbole. To learn some facts about 1956 Chevy performance, *Motor Life* called upon C.J. Hart, for five years head man at the Orange County drag strip in Santa Ana, California. Hart estimated that the number of Chevrolets running there had tripled in the past few years. A 1956 model, equipped with standard transmission, held the stock quarter-mile ac- celeration record at 86.2 mph in the early part of the year; Buick's Century (85 mph) was second, Ford (84.74 mph) was third. The '56 Chevy, Hart said, was a good quarter mph faster than its immediate predecessor with stick shift, and one mph quicker than the '55 with Powerglide which had turned the standing quarter at 81. Again, credit was given to improved engineering: "far fewer Chevrolets are blowing up from the strain of high rpm than last year."

Clymer's *Popular Mechanics* polls tended to add the pub- lic's weight to these opinions from experts. Eighty-five percent of 1956 owners reported no engine trouble at all, against just 65 percent in 1955. Over 80 percent felt the car was "as hot" as Chevy claimed, and the same number felt they needed no more acceleration or top speed. As for the other 20-odd percent, they were probably con- vinced when the 1956 Chevy took to the race tracks.

Returning to Darlington, Mauri Rose took four Yunick- prepared sedans for a 24-hour enduro. A 1956 Two-Ten lapped the 1 3/8-mile track 1773 times in 24 hours, for an average speed of 101.58 mph. This bettered the old U.S. Production Car Class record, previously held by Chrysler, by 11.69 mph. The Chevrolet made 21 pit stops, less than

Plymouth took to performance trail with 1956 Fury.

one an hour, for tires, fuel and driver changes--it went through six drivers in the 24 hour period.

In July, Chevy repeated its Pikes Peak hill climb showing with three cars prepared at Chevrolet Engineering in Warren, Michigan under Vince Piggins' direction. This was Piggins' first official project with Chevrolet after leaving the now defunct Hudson-American Motors performance activity which he headed from 1951 through 1955. The three engineering prepared Chevys were driven by Unser, Korf, and Teague. Chevy placed first, second, fifth, sixth and tenth, with Jerry Unser in the lead car scoring 16.08.0 for the climb, one minute and 16 seconds *better* than Duntov's 1955 record.

STOCK CAR RESULTS

1. Jerry Unser Jr.	1956 Chevrolet	16.08.0
2. Bob Korf	1956 Chevrolet	16.21.6
3. Herb Bryers	1956 Plymouth	16.24.1
4. Chuck Stevenson	1956 Ford	16.27.1
5. Nick Sanborn	1956 Chevrolet	16.31.3
6. Marshall Teague	1956 Chevrolet	16.37.2
7. Johnny Mantz	1956 Ford	16.38.2
8. Dan Morgan	1956 Ford	16.42.8
9. Royal Russel	1956 Plymouth	16.49.2
10. Malcolm Brazier	1956 Chevrolet	17.24.6

Truly, Chevrolet had come a long way in the past two years. In the autumn of 1954, it led Ford by only 19,603 units, 0.36 percent of total production. In 1955 it was 65,000 units ahead, 0.82 percent. When the 1956 figures were totaled, Chevrolet was found to have been ahead of Ford *each month* by more than the sum total of its 1954 lead of 20,000 cars. Despite an industry-wide production tail-off, Chevy's decrease was minimal and its market share actually rose from 23.04 to 27.94 percent.

In a family of three, the 1955-57 Chevy family, the 1956 model was the typical "middle child." It was not considered as spectacular as the 1955, which had been "all new" in both styling and engineering. That, of course, would have been impossible. It was not the end of an era, nor was it the beginning of one. But like "middle children," it had much going for it and didn't necessarily receive the attention it deserved. This was true then, it remains true today: the 1956 is the "least collectable" among the highly collectable 1955-57 Chevrolets.

But 1956 was a key year. It laid important groundwork for what was to come. It was perhaps the most challenging, and in many ways the most interesting year in the 36-month reign of the three most outstanding postwar

UNITED STATES NEW
PASSENGER CAR REGISTRATON, 1956

Chevrolet 6	646,015
Chevrolet V-8	915,880
Corvette V-8	3,504
Total	1,565,399
Ford 6	161,750
Ford V-8	1,197,118
Thunderbird V-8	16,475
Total	1,375,343
Plymouth 6	175,402
Plymouth V-8	308,354
Total	483,756

Chevies. As 1956 passed momentously into 1957, Clare MacKichan's words about the '55 were again to become appropriate: "The car was made to do it...the engine was made to do it... and we did it."

The 1957 Bel Air convertible, foreground, with a prototype or proposal for the 1957 Two-Ten sport sedan that was not adopted.

CHAPTER FOUR

1957:One Horsepower Per Cubic Inch

Nineteen fifty-seven witnessed more tension over Russia and civil rights. Early in January, the Eisenhower Doctrine was formally applied to favor Middle Eastern nations requesting aid from what they saw as Communist aggression. By September, Central High School in Little Rock, Arkansas, had become the nation's battleground, with violence involving the enrollment of nine blacks. President Eisenhower dispatched 1000 paratroopers to quell the chaos.

On the entertainment front, things were more pleasant. Theatre-goers were raving over Leonard Bernstein's "West Side Story" and Meredith Willson's "The Music Man." Oscars were bestowed on "The Bridge on the River Kwai" and actor Alec Guinness. Pat Boone lulled the country with "Love Letters in the Sand;" Elvis shook to "Jailhouse Rock." Philadelphia's finest, M.C. Dick Clark, hooked up coast-to-coast in August, as TV's "American Bandstand" became an overnight tradition.

In sports, the New York Giants and Brooklyn Dodgers forsook Gotham for the west coast, leaving only the Yankees to represent New York in major league baseball--and the indomitable Yanks lost the World Series to the Milwaukee Braves, four games to three. Records were set at opposite ends of the speed spectrum: Major A.E. Drew flew an F-101 Voodoo at an unbelievable 1207.6 mph, and the Mayflower II, duplicating the voyage of the Pilgrims, landed in Plymouth, Massachusetts 54 days after setting out from Plymouth, England.

The biggest news of the year, however, undoubtedly came from the Soviet Union. On October 4th, the Russians launched Sputnik, the first earth satellite, simultaneously launching the United States on an all-out space program of its own, one which eventually caught up and passed Moscow's and saw American astronauts land on the moon.

A little more down to earth, but immensely important in its own right, was a different kind of milestone, another in a long line of credits to Chevrolet Division of General Motors: Chevy became the first American production car to achieve one horsepower from every cubic inch of engine displacement in its new 283 cubic-inch V-8.

Scientific achievements aside--for the moment--1957

The big news for 1957: one hp per cubic inch and fuel injection, as announced in Hot Rod *and* Motor Trend.

posed a pretty big question mark for financial planners in the Motor City. If 1955 had been a banner year, 1956 hadn't given Detroit much more to wave than a pennant. While publicly announcing some $2 billion in capital outlays for 1957 alone, the moguls were quietly hoping that renewed prosperity had really arrived--all across the boards.

Though most 1957 models had been announced by November of 1956, December 8th marked the official blast-off for an industry-wide revival: the National Automobile Show. It was slated for New York's brand new Coliseum, and it was an event not seen in the United States since 1940. In a salute to the car-traveling public, as well as hopeful encouragement to itself, the manufacturers adopted a brave new slogan: "America is on the move!"

"There has always been something reassuring for buyers in the willingness of competitors to stand their products alongside all others in a frank bid for favor," said *The Saturday Evening Post.* Stand together they did--Harold Churchill of Studebaker-Packard, Harlow Curtice of GM, Henry Ford II of Ford, Tex Colbert of Chrysler, and George Romney of American Motors. The Coliseum's three main floors overflowed with 124 models displayed by these companies, plus 66 trucks representing 11 truck manufacturers. General admission was 90 cents, but the whole extravaganza cost between $10 and $12 million.

Unlike auto shows of recent past, "America on the Move" was bereft of dream cars. But newness was emphasized, by such as Virgil Exner's befinned Plymouth Fury and Chrysler 300-C, two super-exotic, super-hot specials from the Number Three manufacturer; American Motors' Rambler with Bendix electronic fuel injection (the unit, alas, never went into production); the bechromed Mercury Turnpike Cruiser; the late-introduction 1957 Packard, in effect not a Packard at all but a jazzed-up, long-wheelbase Studebaker. General Motors chimed in with a fuel-injection Pontiac (later available for dealers only) and a Cadillac Eldorado Brougham with air suspension on all four wheels, which debuted on the showroom floors in February. It was a very complete show, from the practical heavy movers of White, Mack and Diamond T to a frivolous white convertible upholstered with 200 ermine skins--plus the stage show, a 30 minute Broadway musical review, repeated six times daily.

This was the 42nd National Automobile Show, after a 16-year hiatus; the first one was held in 1900, and had continued yearly, undaunted by World War I and Depression, until it halted for World War II after 1940. The first show appeared during the infancy of the automobile, as well as the sponsoring one-year-old Automobile Club of

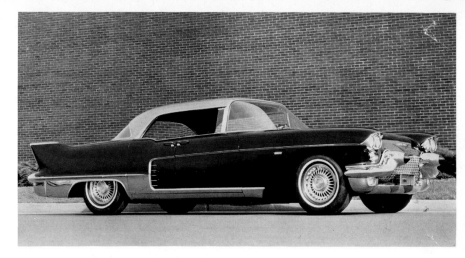

Production Eldorado Brougham used Town Car, Park Avenue ideas.

America, at the original Madison Square Garden. Col. Jacob Astor, later to go down aboard the *Titanic*, and railroad magnate William K. Vanderbilt were among those viewing the 300 cars on display, dominated by steamers and electrics. "America on the Move" was quite a contrast to that.

Harlow Curtice declared the show's overriding goal while in attendance at New York--to usher in another vintage manufacturing year. "The industry in 1957 should produce, and the domestic market absorb, approximately 6,500,000 cars and 900,000 trucks," he said. "Including export, production should approximate 8,300,000 cars and trucks." He was wrong. Production was assuredly up from 1956, but at 7,200,000 cars and trucks it fell considerably short of Curtice's estimates and others. GM's percent of the market actually dropped--from 52.8 to 46.1-- its losses picked up by Ford and Chrysler. This was also reflected at divisional level: Chevrolet dropped from 27.9 to 24.9 percent, Ford rose from 23.7 to 24.9 percent and Plymouth from 7.8 to 10.7 percent.

By June Curtice admitted that 1957 "had not measured up to the industry's expectation. For the second succes-

Limited production Plymouth Fury was another fast package.

From Chrysler: the hot 300-C, with tailfins and much power.

Mercury's Turnpike Cruiser bespoke mid-Fifties kitschwagens.

Packard's 1957 cars were chromey, long-wheelbase Studebakers.

sive year the historical spring rise in sales has failed to materialize." *Time* reported that when asked who was responsible for GM's performance, and present "static styling," Curtice had responded forthrightly: "The present management."

"Static styling" was indeed part of GM's sales problem. Though the Buick, Oldsmobile and Cadillac were redesigned, the bread-and-butter Chevrolet, and Pontiac, wore third year facelifts. These warmed-over designs ran head-

long into a striking new line of Chrysler models by Virgil Exner and a restyled Ford line courtesy George Walker. In 1957 Ford caught Chevrolet in sales; Plymouth had swept back into third place ahead of Buick; Mercury and Dodge were within sight of Pontiac; DeSoto and Chrysler were gaining on Cadillac.

What about the failure of the industry to deliver in general? For one thing, production planners were cautious, burned once by the slow-reducing inventory of 1956 mod-

Ford's innovative retractable hardtop for 1957.

Chevrolet promoted engines from 140 to 283 hp this year.

els. The last quarter of 1956 saw car makers increasing dealer stocks by only 150,000, compared to 280,000 in the fourth quarter of 1955. Slow sales forced a cut in assemblies in the first quarter of 1957, and by the end of March retail stocks were 755,000 cars, compared to 865,000 the previous year.

One New York dealer summed up the general attitude among retailers: "I'm no longer giving away most of my gross just to make a sale...it is better to sell 6 million cars at a reasonable profit than to sell 6.5 million at a small profit or sometimes at no profit at all." Together with a tightening of installment buying credit, and less pressure from the factories, this attitude slowed things down. There was one other factor: "Rear fenders were not the only thing that shot skyward on '57 model cars," said *Wards*. "Prices went up, too." The average factory retail price in 1957 was $2749, against $2553 in 1956, $2300 in 1955.

That all important production battle, The Great Race between Chevy and Ford, was fiercely waged in '57, remind-ing one of '54. As in 1954, who you believed depended on the figures you accepted. In calendar year production Chevrolet led Ford by a mere 130 units (1,522,536 to 1,522,406). But in model year production, Ford had achieved undisputed supremacy, 1,655,068 to 1,552,471. The '57 Chevy was accurately described by *Motor Life:* "Never before has it had so much to offer. And--as a matter of fact--never has it needed it more."

"The only one of the Big Three to resist a complete body change is Chevrolet," reported *Motor Trend*, "and it is by far the best equipped of the lowest price group to do so. With a more than comfortable '56 sales lead over Ford and an unbroken record of winning every sales race for more than 20 years, Chevy can complacently count on coming out ahead once more in '57." Well, Chevy didn't come out ahead and that same issue of *Motor Trend* could indicate why: "Plymouth showrooms are jammed, and with reason. Not since the introduction of the '55 Chevrolet has a car changed so completely." *Fortune* reported a Ford radio spot: "Archie of Duffy's Tavern, appalled to learn that his boss plans to buy a certain new car [by implication a Chevrolet] asked, "Would you marry Mrs. Duffy again just because she had her face lifted?"

Fortunately for Chevrolet, progress had been made under-the-skin which completely overshadowed whatever had been done to the exterior. At the time this was of some help in the showrooms; in retrospect, to the collector or enthusiast, it signified the most desirable postwar Chevrolet passenger car of all: "One Horsepower Per Cubic Inch." Chevy had mated its new 283 cubic inch V-8 with "Ramjet" fuel injection built by Rochester, and offered 10.5:1 compression to attain 283 gross horsepower. It had also introduced a new automatic transmission, Turboglide, along the lines of Buick's Dynaflow.

The Chevy V-8 now offered a range of horsepower from 162 to 283, using the 265 and 283 cid engines. The latter's displacement had been achieved by boring out the block 1/8th inch, to 3.875 inches, and in addition to F.I. and higher compression it featured a higher lift cam, and single or dual four-barrel carburetors. Mechanical valve lifters were used for fuel injection engines, while on other powerplants the hydraulic lifters now received full pressure (instead of metered) lubrication. Longer-reach spark plugs

were used, with metal deflection shields to protect wiring and plug caps from manifold heat. The top of the block was a thicker casting, to discourage cylinder wall distortion via over-tight hold-down bolts. Fuel passages were tapered, increasing in cross-sectional area going toward the inlet ports and in the "ram's horn" exhaust manifold, to provide better scavenging and increased volumetric efficiency. There was a new distributor, with breaker points directly above the shaft bearing, which helped reduce fluctuations in the gap setting. And the front and intermediate main bearings were 1/16th inch thicker.

The hullabaloo over the new 283 overshadowed the continuation of two tried-and-true power units on the 1957 Chevy--the "Blue-Flame" six and the 265 cid V-8. Most changes to the six were necessitated by new styling: the carburetor air cleaner was redesigned, the upper radiator tank was flatter, and the radiator water inlet was moved to the side. All these revisions were necessary because of a lower hood line. One genuine mechanical improvement was a fuel strainer on the inlet side of the carburetor, supplementing the fuel tank filter and reducing the chance of flooding due to foreign material in the carb. Changes were made to the starter and generator, in common with the same units on the V-8s.

The 265 cubic inch V-8 (cam lift .3336-inch) was the base unit against the new 283 (cam lift .3987 inch), but both engines carried as standard a two-barrel, automatic choke carburetor, single exhaust, and hydraulic valve lifters, with full-flow oil filter a mandatory option. The 283 as mentioned earlier, could then be developed upward with a range of power equipment, while the 265 was available only in its basic form. Engineering changes common to both V-8s included carburetor fuel filters, larger ports, wide bearings, stainless steel expander in the oil control rings for closer manufacturing tolerances and better lube control, heat deflection shields to protect spark plug leads, a relocated choke to improve hot starting characteristics. When installed, dual exhausts were provided with a new balance tube, which equalized the exhaust flow through the mufflers and made the life of both exhaust systems approximately equal.

Many other engineering changes were associated with V-8s. While higher torque rating clutches were used on both the 265 and six, whenever manual transmission was specified the 283 used a new semi-centrifugal clutch with either four-barrel carburetor or fuel injection. The 283's new distributor was common also to the 265: there was a relocated voltage regulator and battery, line fuses in lamp circuits when the accessory junction block was not installed. The chassis wiring harness was divided into separate units, interconnected by multi-plugs.

Of course the biggest single engine feature was GM's new fuel injection option on the 283 powerplant. Though of Rochester manufacture, the system was almost entirely designed by GM Engineering Staff, and simplified for production by Harry Barr and Zora Duntov. It consisted of three main components: fuel meter, manifold assembly and air meter. Replacing intake manifold and carburetor, the Ramjet unit took in air first, then injected fuel directly into each intake port for mixing. The amount of injection was very precisely controlled, encouraging improved volumetric efficiency and better fuel economy. Starting and warm-up during cold weather were bettered, and the unit by itself provided about five more horsepower than the same engine with twin four-barrel carburetors. Chevrolet claimed that F.I. eliminated manifold icing, and reduced the tendency to stall when cornering hard.

Since there is no way to improve on the original canned press release description of Ramjet's operation, it is quoted herewith in full. (Letters refer to diagram, next page.)

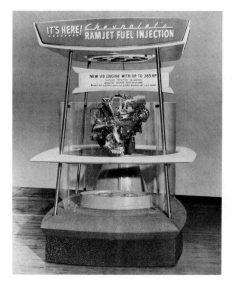

Fuel injection in display case.   *F.I. installation on 283 V-8.*

"When the accelerator pedal is pushed down, the throttle valve (A) is opened, admitting air into the intake manifold. At the same time a signal is sent to the fuel meter so that the air/fuel mixture will be in the proper ratio. Fuel to the system is supplied by a conventional engine fuel pump, and flows through a filter to a fuel bowl (B), controlled by a float system similar to those used in carburetors. The high pressure fuel pump (C), driven by a cable from the distributor, pumps the fuel under pressure to the fuel control valve (D).

"This valve is fundamentally the metering device of the fuel injection system, for through a system of controls tied to it, it determines the amount of fuel that is pumped to the engine. In almost all operation, except wide open throttle, some of the fuel is bypassed and allowed to return to the fuel bowl. The amount of fuel that spills back into the fuel bowl determines the pressure within the fuel valve, which in turn depends on the position of the spill plunger.

"For starting, a solenoid (E) connected to the starter circuit operates to unseat the fuel valve and allow fuel flow past the valve to the nozzles (F) at cranking rpm. When the fuel valve returns to normal, all fuel flows through the center of the valve.

"During warmup, the necessary rich mixtures are provided by blocking the vacuum passage to the enrichment diaphragm (G). This is done by a ball check in the electric choke (H) that remains closed until the coil is heated sufficiently to force a piston to unseat it.

"During idling, when the air flow is so low

that it has little effect on the fuel control diaphragm (J), the venturi signal is strengthened by manifold vacuum through a tube to the enrichment diaphragm. When decelerating, a spring-loaded diaphragm (K) reacts to closed-throttle deceleration vacuum to lift a valve in the high pressure pump outlet, which completely relieves pump pressure so that there is no fuel flow.

"One of the keys to the success of this system is the design of the fuel nozzles. Instead of discharging directly to vacuum, they discharge to atmospheric pressure and the spray (at pressures up to 200 psi) is targeted across an air duct into the manifold just above the intake port. This allows larger orifices, reduced fuel percolation due to vacuum in the fuel lines, and a continuous fuel flow at low rpm."

A special two-piece aluminum manifold casting was used on 283 V-8s equipped with fuel injection. The upper casting contained air passages and the air-fuel metering system bases, while the lower casting made up ram tubes and covered the top center of the engine.

Chevrolet predicted little servicing problems for the injection unit, since the only potentially troublesome electrical unit was the (replaceable) solenoid. On the off chance that any dirt got by both fuel line and plunger filters, a mechanic needed only to remove the clogged nozzle and blow it out with air. The eight nozzles came in sets, and Chevrolet warned that any replacements be from sets of the same coding. In practice, it wasn't quite as painless as this--of which more later.

Chevy's other major engineering innovation for 1957 was its new automatic transmission, Turboglide, available optionally on the 283 cid V-8 only. (Three-speed manual, manual overdrive and Powerglide were available as before).

Annotated diagram of fuel injection system, from Motor Trend.

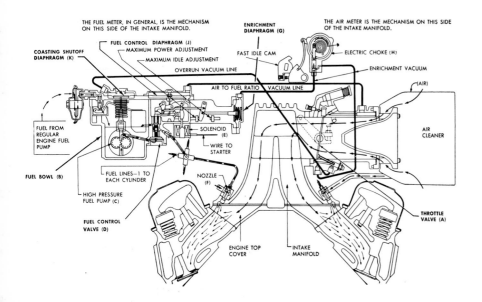

Lighter by 82 pounds than Powerglide, it embodied three turbines and two planetary gearsets, in combination with variable pitch stator and the conventional torque converter pump. Engine power was translated into road motion by turbine rotation through the oil in the torque converter pump. Which pump started to rotate depended on the position of its vanes; as the turning force of the first turbine decreased, the second began to rotate, driving its shaft and the output shaft through the rear planetary gearset, and on to the third turbine in succession. Ultimately all three turbines free-wheeled as the car gathered speed.

Turboglide embodied a passing gear through its variable pitch stator which, on floor-boarding, increased its blade angle to deliver greater torque to the output shaft. The Turboglide quadrant included a position labeled "HR" for "Hill Retarder," which took the position on the extreme right and acted to slow a car when descending steep hills. Its value in acceleration was nil, since it operated by creating turbulence of the oil of the torque converter to induce a drag on the rear wheels.

Rear axles and brakes were also revised this year. The new axle ratios were 3.36:1 for automatic, 3.55:1 for manual, and the same 4.11:1 for overdrive. New facing material, less sensitive to temperature change, was applied to the front brake linings, and the front secondary brake shoe pull-back springs were increased from 40 to 50 pound rate. Coil-type springs replaced clip-types on all brake shoes.

From a mechanical standpoint, fuel injection, the 283 V-8 and Turboglide were the main newsmakers for 1957. The basic chassis remained at 115 inches wheelbase, though the frame was beefed up with new front crossmember-to-sidemember braces and the length of the cars grew to almost 17 feet. New power control-arm ball joint and seal assemblies were used in the front suspension, and the shock absorbers were revised in accord with new chassis

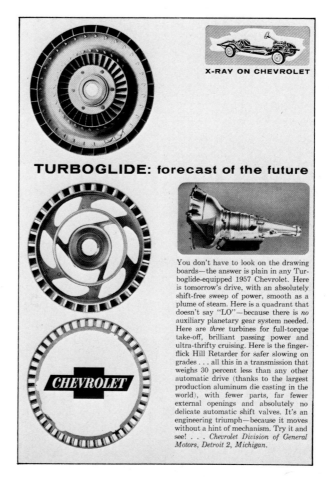

X-RAY ON CHEVROLET

TURBOGLIDE: forecast of the future

You don't have to look on the drawing boards—the answer is plain in any Turboglide-equipped 1957 Chevrolet. Here is tomorrow's drive, with an absolutely shift-free sweep of power, smooth as a plume of steam. Here is a quadrant that doesn't say "LO"—because there is *no* auxiliary planetary gear system needed. Here are *three* turbines for full-torque take-off, brilliant passing power and ultra-thrifty cruising. Here is the finger-flick Hill Retarder for safer slowing on grades . . . all this in a transmission that weighs 30 percent less than any other automatic drive (thanks to the largest production aluminum die casting in the world), with fewer parts, far fewer external openings and absolutely no delicate automatic shift valves. It's an engineering triumph—because it moves without a hint of mechanism. Try it and see! . . . *Chevrolet Division of General Motors, Detroit 2, Michigan.*

New Turboglide supplemented two-speed Powerglide.

weight requirements. The rear leaf springs were moved further outboard to improve roadholding. Following an industry trend, Chevrolet switched to 14-inch tires, which ran a lower pressure (22 psi). None of these changes were very visible, though the car itself lacked not for visibility: it was, in fact, a substantial facelift, and a rather successful one.

Chassis assembly began by welding sub-components to frame.

Front springs are fitted with the aid of hydraulic presses.

Engine is emplaced after suspension has been installed.

Roof is positioned before being spot-welded to main body.

...e body drop: a Two-Ten two door meets chassis/running gear.

Finished seats are ready for installation as bodies approach.

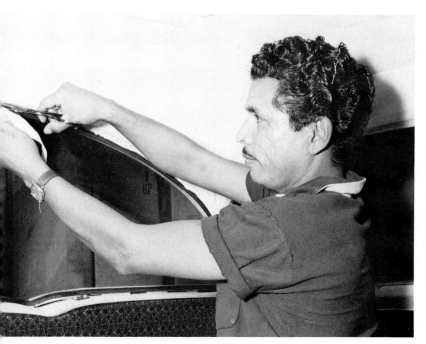

...rker carefully trims fabric headliner for accurate fitting.

End of the line: finished cars roll toward final inspection.

Ram's horn exhaust manifolds are visible in view of 283 engine.

Engine compartment for '57 was slightly more cramped than '56.

The facelift assignment for 1957 was, of course, one with absolute boundaries. The paramount need, to make do with the basic shell of the '55, was generally accepted by Styling Staff. "It wasn't a bad move," says Clare Mac-Kichan in thinking back. "We just had no choice, we had to carry the line out until 1958...a three year facelift we *had* to do. I guess probably that is why we did some of the things we did on the '57. We were as extreme as we could be, while saving the deck, roof and doors. Those were the established ground rules. As I recall, there was a great deal of pressure on us in the Chevrolet studio [to add distinction to] the '57 car."

The author naturally asked MacKichan what effect the styling of Chrysler's Exner, who so drastically altered the appearance of the 1955 Chrysler products, had on Chevrolet. Chevy's former styling chief's reply was predictable. The competition's ideas, he said, were always being consid-

ered: "We always have to be ahead of our competition, no matter what they do or how much money they spend. So what we were supposed to do [on the 1957 Chevy] was ...beat Chrysler and Ford but not change the basic shape of the thing. We did manage to get entirely new graphics in the front, and the back was pretty different looking, too. We did such obvious things as moving taillights to a new location, changing that whole corner. From the side we did a similar thing with the aluminum panel and trim molding. We just did everything we could to change those cars, within the ground rules that we were stuck with." Chrysler's influence, MacKichan concluded, was slight insofar as it effected the '57 Chevrolet: "It did have an effect on what was done afterwards, in 1958 or 1959." One must remember that the '57 was in the works before Exner's all new 1955 designs appeared, and two years before the scintillating "Forward Look, '57."

As MacKichan says, frontal graphics were entirely new, but what the designers ultimately evolved did not appear overnight. A massive bumper surrounding a concave grille had been evident in styling sketches as early as 1949, and possibly earlier if one includes the huge 1949-50 Buick's grille, with concave vertical teeth, as part of the same family. As early as 1953 the same idea can be traced to the Chevrolet program, as witness the rendering by Carl Renner on these pages. Of this theme, Renner recalled that "Mr. MacKichan guided his men into this. We went all the way with our designs...and then backed off. You never can get criticized for going way out, but you always can be criticized for the lack of imagination, for not going far enough. We went that far in 1953, and early in the [1955-

The production 1957 bumper-grille was clearly evolving at the time of this clay model, May, 1954. The idea partly stemmed from the sketch below, by Carl Renner in 1953.

57] program. Finally, when they had money to do something quite radical for Chevrolet, we went into this bumper grille. I remember, Mac pushed that concept, and went into it, finally, for '57."

The 1957 front end *was* radical, one of those things whose absence on the first generation 1955 Chevy is easy to understand. Said MacKichan, "That was one hell of a thing we had to go through to get these bumpers, because you can see the difference between [its] cost and that of the '56. It was *tremendous*. And I guess that is the kind of thing you can do on a facelift year. You can spend a little bit more money."

Every detail of the '57 was styled for a lower, longer appearance. The new Chevy was 2½ inches longer, 1½ in-

ches lower, and benefited from its new 14-inch wheels and wider, lower pressure tires. A new ventilation system, removing the air intakes from the cowl vent to screened scoops in the upper half of the headlamp bezels, also helped reduce the car's height. The intakes were connected to the car's interior through long, concealed ducts emptying into the firewall.

Absence of cowl ventilation allowed a lower, flatter hood, which was dressed up with twin "lance-shaped windsplits" to replace a conventional hood ornament. (The things were custom made for the amateur restyle artists prevalent in those years, and soon '57 Chevies were sprouting all manner of hood mods from amber auxiliary running lights to reversed '59 Cadillac taillights.) All of this

Dual hooded headlights and concave grille with vertical bars are features of late 1954 prototype, which was 1957 proposal.

was fronted with the new bumper/grille, a ponderous, full-width structure with integral bumper guards and an aluminum center screen set off by a horizontal bar containing the parking lamps. That this feature had been subject to the most rigorous decision-making is evidenced by the large number of clay models in Chevrolet files, showing all sorts of alternatives: inset hood ornaments, hooded headlamps, variations on concave eggcrate grille themes, even heavy bar type grilles. The end result was an entirely new look, though the price was a steep one and the overall frontal appearance, compared to 1955-56, "heavy."

Along the flanks the design objective was to retain the 1955-56 door and roof boundaries while creating a look that was definitely new--no small order. Styling Staff's so-

lution was simple, and brilliantly effective. In every model, from One-Fifty to Bel Air, side decoration was accomplished by discreet flashes of brightwork: a combination of vertical and horizontal bars on the rear half of the One-Fifty; a straight-through bar, gracefully dipped toward the rear, splitting into a forward-pointed triangle under the rear side windows on the Two-Ten and Bel Air. The areas created by these trims on One-Fifty and Two-Ten allowed the use of two tones which, by modern standards, hampered the overall look of the car, but that was a decision prompted by the sales requisites of the time. However, the '57 side trims remain among the best facelift ideas in an era given over to more slap-happy approaches elsewhere.

In production, Two-Tens had the rear "triangle" filled

From rear, same clay model bore Nomad script (probably for placement only) but almost unaltered rear end styling.

Tail end appliqué not selected used horizontal striping.

with a second color when two-toned, while Bel Airs used an attractive ribbed brushed aluminum panel. But an interesting paradox surrounds these two treatments: in early promotional literature an entirely different approach was illustrated. The Two-Tens were displayed with just the single, major, front-to-rear molding bar, and a yellow and ivory Bel Air hardtop with a painted (instead of brushed aluminum) triangle!

The explanation for the change from this first trim arrangement to the production version is simple: late in the game, Harley Earl came up with the brushed aluminum panel for the Bel Air. This allowed the Bel Air's painted panel to be applied down-line, on the Two-Ten. Clare MacKichan provided the explanation and, as he notes, "that was a pretty high bill that they had to pay." But the effectiveness of the new Bel Air panel was indisputable. Harley Earl had long admired brushed aluminum, stainless steel, titanium and other metals and alloys as dress-up materials --as evidenced by his Motorama cars.

Another interesting innovation on 1957 Chevrolets was the three-louver trim on the front fenders: depressions only on One-Fifties and Two-Tens, but capped with gold-anodized aluminum on Bel Airs. MacKichan remembers the origin of this feature too: "Harley Earl was responsible for that. He was a great believer in details. *Interest*, he called it. 'You've got to have interest in a car,' he would say. And it seemed like we got more *interest* as we went along." (More *interest* appeared in 1958, with the advent of no less than four such simulated louvers.)

From the rear, the new line was also quite different and, in the opinion of many, greatly improved. Rear quarter panels were altered to incorporate modest fins to accentuate the new low lines. Sales brochures trumpeted this feature: "rakish new high-set rear fenders swept down to form a unit combining tail, stop and directional signal lights, bumper guard, and space for accessory backup lights. A panel in the left fender molding swings aside to reveal the fuel filler cap!" Designers originally planned to exit the exhaust from an oval port in the bumper end, beneath the taillamp, but as MacKichan explained, "Cadillac found that this dirtied up the bumper considerably, and it was changed in the middle of the design. Toward the last of the design period, we put optional back-up lights in that area."

Relative to the new Ford and Plymouth, the press found Chevrolet's 1957 styling "moderately conservative," despite the extreme efforts employed to update the package. The '57 Chevy reflected GM's familial relationship in a Buick-Olds look at the front end, a Cadillac treatment at the rear. Still, as Carl Renner puts it, "the design was very rare and unusual for Chevrolet. The bumper/grille was quite unique, the side treatment and fins were bold. The taillamp sort of integrated with the rear bumper. For Chevrolet, it had a massive and strong look--quite a departure from the '55.

...rice leader for 1957: the One-Fifty utility sedan at $1985.

The One-Fifty two-door sedan, of which 70,774 were built.

...he four-door One-Fifty actually sold less—only 52,000 units.

The Handyman two-door, six passenger wagon, One-Fifty series.

Very sleek and clean, but uncommon: The Two-Ten sport coupe.

The Two-Ten two-door sedan, priced at $2222, saw 162,000 units.

Neat styling was evident on the One-Fifty sedan delivery.

The Two-Ten four-door sedan, a popular and high-volume model.

The four-door Two-Ten sport sedan: *most preferred Bel Airs.*

Seating nine passengers, the Two-Ten Beauville station wagon.

The Delray club coupe in the Two-Ten series saw 25,000 units.

Six-passenger two-door Two-Ten wagon was the Handyman model.

Today a leading collectable, the Bel Air two-door sport coupe.

At $2338, Bel Air two-door sedan exceeded 60,000 production.

Four-door top line hardtop Bel Air, which sold 137,670 units.

Unmatched for good looks was the pretty Bel Air convertible.

Furry lady and toothy friend like the Bel Air Townsman wagon.

Late '56 Corvette with non-standard tires, a '57 press photo.

"The people that bought Chevrolets, like myself, naturally had the feeling of wanting to own a Cad some day. Looking back, I think it was our [Styling Staff's] objective to make a Chevrolet look like a 'little Cadillac.' Why *not* give people who could afford a Chevrolet that Cadillac look of quality? And I thought it was a good deal. I think that is one reason why Chevrolet sold so well."

Appearing in 19 body styles and the usual One-Fifty, Two-Ten and Bel Air series, the 1957 Chevrolet made its showroom debut on October 17th, 1956. The only model change was the replacement of the nine-passenger Beauville Bel Air wagon with a six-passenger Townsman. Numerous power team choices were available, and the cars could be had in 16 solid and 15 two-tone color combinations depending on series and body style.

While national advertising proclaimed the attainment of

"the engineer's dream...One H.P. Per Cubic Inch," sales brochures dwelled on the restyling job, calling the Chevy "sweet, smooth and sassy," promoting not only the exterior changes but the interior revisions--which were considerable. A redesigned "flight panel" featured an instrument cluster grouped so as to be plainly visible through the "tailored steering wheel with its safety-styled, recessed hub and off-centered spokes." Control knobs were "finger-tip close, set deeply in a cover for added safety and smartness." A major improvement was the placement of the radio speaker centrally under a grid on the upper dash, instead of in the dashboard itself. This meant that the speaker no longer blared out directly at the passenger, and the sound was more audible for the driver. Unfortunately, it also meant that speakers wore out faster, being subject to the intense light and heat of that particular location.

Seats and door panels wore a new treatment, in both design and material. Two-Tens used a patterned cloth combined with textured vinyl except for the Delray interior, which was all-vinyl. Bel Airs were dressed in Jacquard-loomed cloth combined with vinyl, and Bel Air floors were carpeted.

As before, there were exterior differences to distinguish the three lines from each other, and the sixes from the V-8s. Hoods and decks on the latter carried Chevrolet script with a wide "V" underneath; sixes wore the plain script up front, and a Chevrolet emblem on the deck. Whereas the two lower models used silver anodized aluminum for grille mesh and identification trim, Bel Airs relied heavily on gold: on the grille mesh, hood decoration, fender louvers, and rear deck accents.* Six cylinder models wore their identifying trim in gold: Chevrolet script on hood, an emblem on the deck. Bright metal body sill moldings were standard on the 1957 Bel Air, as were full disc wheel covers--though whitewalls remained optional. Bel Air detailing was considerable this year, an obvious attempt to add as much *interest* as possible in this third-year facelift.

Optional equipment across the boards included power steering ($70), power brakes ($54), electric window lifts ($59/102) and power seats ($43). Factory air conditioning was available at $425, less than in 1956. The transmission options pegged Turboglide at $231 extra, Powerglide $188, overdrive $108. Fuel injection was a costly $550.

With Ford and Plymouth all-new for 1957, Chevrolet's facelift didn't provoke many comments, and what did appear was mixed. "The bumpers offer good protection," Floyd Clymer wrote, "[and are] more economical to re-

pair in event of damage." *Motor Trend* wondered if the new fender vent ducts would "give trouble when they clog with winter ice and slush," and said they were "in a position that has been generally discredited because of exhaust fumes in close traffic." *MT* was pretty far afield in this criticism: in close traffic the ram effect on any air duct is absent, and the only way to clog these high, well-protected ducts with ice and slush would be to pack it on manually and let it freeze overnight. The placement of the ducts in the headlamp bezels also contributed to longer fender life, since they acted as a baffle to prevent dirt and moisture from building up in the small area between the fender and headlamp housing. No similar protection existed in 1955 and 1956, and as restorers know, deterioration in that area is common. The duct placement may have originated with Styling Staff, but it was enormously practical as a longevity factor.

Clever air intake surrounded 1957 cars' headlights.

---

* Early Bel Airs had gold plated emblems and scripts on hood and deck lid. After approximately November 1st, these parts were made from gold anodized aluminum, less expensive and more durable.

Motor Trend did speak favorably of the engine compartment, calling it "one of the cleanest we've seen...An enormous space in front of the radiator is useless, but you can get around the compact V-8 with refreshing ease." Plugs, however, were inaccessible--more difficult to get to than in 1955-56. *MT* condemned the 1957 taillights as too low and accident prone. No survey was ever taken as to the effect of their lowness, and their smaller size may have actually been an advantage over the gigantic taillights on other cars, which could be a blinding distraction to following traffic.

There was disagreement on the degree of craftsmanship displayed. *Motor Life*, for example, praised Chevy quality. "It can't be missed, even in the most casual inspection... The materials are sound and substantial, with precision finish abundantly evident...Everything was as tight and solid as could be expected." But *Motor Trend* again wasn't happy: "A poorly hung rear door whose window was extremely tough to roll down, uneven paint on the dash molding, and badly fitting bright-work on the dash itself, marred the looks of the test car." *MT* did admit that such details would probably improve as production increased.

The 1957 interior was generally praised. *Motor Life* found the instruments readable and devoid of reflections. *Motor Trend* approved the centrally-located glove compartment (a particular quest of road testers everywhere in the middle Fifties) and a distortion-free wrap-around windshield, noting that both these conveniences were lacking in the Ford and Plymouth. *Consumer Reports* liked the lower cowl and improved forward vision, though *MT* found that its dashboard-mounted rearview mirror blocked the right front fender for shorter drivers* and Floyd Clymer

* Although rearview mirrors were centrally located atop the windshield, on the upper reveal molding, brochures show dash-mounted mirrors on Two-Ten and Bel Air sport coupes and sport sedans.

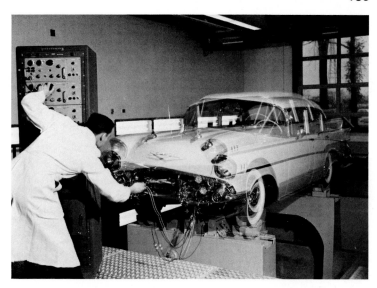

Sedan body is checked for rigidity on stress testing machine.

Pre-production components are tested for correct size and fit.

was annoyed by a full-circle horn ring. Everybody thought the rear fins aided parking, but nobody, thankfully, said they aided stability at 150 mph. The fact of a three-year-old body style was an advantage in one area: headroom. Clymer said Chevy was "one of the few 1957 cars in which the tall driver can wear a hat."

The new front end *looked* heavy, and before driving the car many pressmen were speculating that the handling would be effected. It was. *Motor Trend*, which had awarded Chevrolet the "best-handling" award for 1955-56, found "greater lean on corners, and less confidence for the driver [due to] cancelling out some of its advantages by going to a somewhat softer ride...Personally, we prefer the taut feel of the '56." They did, but the customers obviously didn't. The Chevrolet ride was improved from a softness standpoint, though the advantages gained were questionable given the excessive lean encountered on all but the mildest corners by most testers. "Chevrolet handling falls below the standard set the previous year," concluded *Motor Life*.

Drum brakes will be drum brakes, and the 1957 Chevy's were no exception. While *Consumer Reports* found braking favorable, *CR* was never known for driving very hard. Floyd Clymer encountered fade on sharp grades, *Motor Trend* said the brakes were "inadequate for mountain driving or highway [driving] with traffic...Pedal pressure be-

MOTOR TREND PREPARED THIS CHART COMPARING 1956-57 PERFORMANCE.

1956

Acceleration

(205 bhp engine)

From Standing Start
0-30 mph 4.2 0-60 mph 10.7
Quarter mile 18.3 and 76 mph
Passing Speeds
30-50 mph 3.9 50-80 mph 12.0

Fuel Consumption

Used Mobilgas Special
Steady Speeds
20.8 mph @ 30 19.4 mpg @ 45
16.6 mpg @ 60 13.6 mpg @ 75
Stop-and-Go Driving
14.2 mpg tank average for 800 miles

1957

Acceleration

(270 bhp engine)

From Standing Start
0-45 mph 6.75 0-60 mph 9.9
Quarter-mile 17.5 and 77.5 mph
Passing Speeds
30-50 mph 3.55 45-60 mph 2.9
50-80 mph 9.9

Fuel Consumption

Used Mobilgas Special
Steady Speeds
16.75 mpg @ 30 14.8 mpg @ 45
13.1 mpg @ 60 12.2 mpg @ 75
Stop-and-Go Driving
13.6 mpg tank average for 136 miles
Highway Driving
15.0 mpg tank average for 312 miles

gan to increase on sixth stop, continued through tenth stop. Impossible to hold 15 feet per second rate on eighth and ninth stops." It seems incredible that the brilliant engineers who had given us one horsepower per cubic inch couldn't seem to do anything to improve on the time-honored drum brake, by now being fast-outstripped by the performance capability of automobiles. For Chevrolet, as for many others, the drum had become like the old joke about the V-1 rocket: They couldn't fire it, and couldn't get it to work.

Chevrolet's forte in 1957 was, of course, straight line performance. While the best lightfooted *Consumer Re-*

ports could wring out of the 185 hp V-8 was 0-60 in 13.6 seconds, *Motor Life* produced a more typical 11 seconds flat. Then, taking up a 270 hp Powerglide version, *ML* recorded 8.2 seconds, and concluded that Chevy was the hottest of the low-priced three on a model-for-model, dollar-for dollar basis. *Motor Trend's* performance chart, reproduced on these pages, also put Chevrolet's acceleration times at the top of its class.

But acceleration, by now, was an expected feature of Chevrolet V-8s, and what buyers were anxious to discover this year was the benefits of those two new developments, Turboglide transmission and fuel injection. Turboglide, it

1957 PERFORMANCE

Make, Model and Horsepower	Chevrolet Bel Air 4D HT 270 BHP	Ford Fairlane 4D SED 245 BHP	Plymouth Belvedere CONV 290 BHP
Acceleration Time in Seconds:			
0—45 mph	6.8	6.9	6.9
0—60 mph	9.9	11.1	11.5
¼ mile	17.5	18.2	17.7
¼ mile speed (mph)	77.5	77.0	77.0
30—50 mph	3.6	4.3	4.3
45—60 mph	2.9	4.3	4.6
50—80 mph	9.9	12.4	14.9
Fuel Consumption in Mpg: *			
Steady Speeds			
30 mph	16.8	20.6	—
45 mph	14.8	17.0	—
60 mph	13.1	14.2	—
75 mph	12.2	13.6	—
Tank Average	15.0	15.6	13.5
Stops Before Brake Fade **	5	7	—

*Incomplete data indicates full-scale road tests were not conducted.
** Stops are made at deceleration rate of 15 ft/sec^2 from 60 to 20 mph until fade is encountered.

Motor Trend *performance chart compared Chevrolet and its two closest competitors.*

If handling had worsened, the '57 ads didn't notice!

The dashing new Corvette (left) and the Bel Air Sport Coupe.

Basking in Corvette glory really wasn't necessary.

seems, was universally lauded. "Almost turbine smooth," wrote Ken Fermoyle of *Motor Life*, "perhaps the smoothest automatic I've ever run across. From standstill up through the speed range, there was never a balk, jerk or anything else to indicate it even had a transmission hooked to the engine!" Said Walt Woron and Pete Molson of *Motor Trend*, "we heartily recommend it...as satisfying a transmission as any automatic we've driven." Wrote Woron, "Once I put the quadrant in drive, I noticed absolutely no upshifting sensation. The only feeling you get

that's at all like a shift is that if you suddenly lift your foot from the throttle while you're still accelerating, the blade angle of the variable stator as quickly changes. You then get an imperceptibly smooth shift." Woron also liked the Chevy hill retarder. "Going down a 17 percent grade, I dropped it into HR which immediately slowed it down from 40 to 20 mph...the slowing action was exceedingly quick--just like shifting down a manual gearbox. Highest recommended speed for downshifting is 40 mph, though the engineers told me that they do it consistently at 55."

Woron and Molson ran stopwatch performance checks, did 0–60 in 10.1 seconds, and pronounced the '57 "appreciably faster on all counts" than the Powerglide '56.

Consumer Reports staged an interesting comparison test between Turboglide, Fordomatic and TorqueFlite, noticing definite shifts from one set of planetary gears to another on the last two. But Turboglide "makes no shifts at all: one torque converter, driving through a set of gears, is succeeded as vehicle speed increases by a second unit with lower-ratio gears, and it by a third converter acting alone. The changes could not be felt, though at times an audible whine of differing pitch distinguished one converter-and-gear from another."

By 1961, Turboglide was gone, almost as suddenly as it had arrived. How so, if according to these glowing reports, it was so successful? Vince Piggins puts it like this: "We had the Powerglide, which was a very successful transmission, and we also had the Hydra-Matic which not only GM, but American Motors was using. So there was really very little need of another transmission, and it was expensive to build. It wasn't as economical as the Hydra-Matic, because it was a two-speed, much like the Buick Dynaflow. That went the way of the Turboglide because it was a high-slip torque converter, very smooth, but not as efficient as the Hydra-Matic."

In retrospect, Piggins thinks, "It would have taken a few more years to really get Turboglide to the reliability stage that the Hydra-Matic already achieved, and sales being what they were, it just didn't make sense."

As for fuel injection, the road testers found it hard to come by.* *Consumer Reports* publicly gave up trying to

---

* The National Corvette Restorers Society has documented the fact that 1040 of 6338 1957 Corvettes were equipped with fuel injection. NCRS suggests to the author that the approximate total of fuel injected 1957 Chevrolet cars was 1530.

obtain a F.I. car. *Motor Trend* said in August 1957 that "only a midget's handful of citizens are making payments on fuel injected cars...And agencies with a F.I. Chevy for sale are the envy of their business associates." *Motor Life*, which managed to test an F.I. Corvette, noted that the option "has created a furor which has the engineers burning the midnight oil, the ad agencies looking for new adjectives and the ultimate buyer completely confused."

Some 20 years later, exhaustive research by the writer has unearthed only *one* source reporting on driving a 1957 fuel injected Chevrolet passenger car--and that was a brief, sketchy and disheartening one. But a few pieces do fall together, and the following is at least a partial explanation of the mystique surrounding F.I. in the Chevrolet car.

A major engineering development is never simple--or easy. Chevy's introduction of Rochester fuel injection was a milestone among production cars, but bugs were inevitable. As *Motor Trend* reported, at the Daytona National Speed Weeks, "the much heralded fuel cutoff during ac-

Tom McCahill and Zora Duntov check fuel injected 1957 Corvette.

celeration has been eliminated because someone concluded that shutting off fuel created an objectionable flat spot in acceleration response. Another change in Chevrolet's set-up has been lengthening of the fuel nozzles. They used to absorb enough heat to cause rough idling. Now, nozzles extend further into the air stream for cooling."

To be sure, these were *initial* bugs, and once cleared of them the F.I. unit was remarkably trouble-free. Unfortunately, when it did need maintenance very few mechanics were trained to service it. "I, for one," said Tom McCahill, "am wondering about getting such a gadget serviced in the badlands of Black Bearskin, Dakota."

Vince Piggins indicates that there was truth to McCahill's observation. Servicing at Daytona Speed Weeks in February, 1957, was pretty complicated: "It was a very complex unit, very prone to dirt, clogging, dirty fuel, and what not, and we did not have the mechanical expertise in the field to readily handle that type of unit. Even when we used it in racing, we didn't bother fixing them at the track. We carried extra ones, that were already rebuilt, in cellophane bags in a box. We changed the whole unit. We didn't attempt to service them there because they had to be set up and metered on a flow bench to determine that you had the proper pressure and the proper fuel flow. Repair by replacement. That's how we handled it."

Since F.I. Corvette tests are the only available source of information, it is interesting to dwell on the performance they recorded. Consistently, from car to car, 0–60 times of the highest hp versions averaged just over six seconds, and top speeds in the neighborhood of 140 mph. With a 250 hp F.I. Corvette, 33 hp below the 1957 maximum, Walt Woron ran the 0–60 sprint in just 7.2 seconds. With Zora Duntov's special 283 hp version, 10.5:1 heads, dual exhaust, special cam and solid lifters, he did 134 mph and was convinced that the car wasn't extended. Extrapolat-

ing, a two-door Chevrolet sedan weighing approximately 400 pounds more might--all else being equal, which is a big assumption--do 0–60 in just less than eight seconds and have a top speed of over 120 mph with the right rear axle gearing. If that's true, the run of two-doors with F.I. units dropped in by the St. Louis assembly plant, in preparation for the Daytona Speed Weeks, must have culminated in a rather quick bunch of automobiles.

But whatever it did for performance, fuel injection just didn't seem to fly--in the marketplace or with the road testers. In mid-1957, *Motor Trend* summed up a 5000-mile study with four different cars--a Daytona Chevy two-door "9000 miles and six clutches later," a "jumpy blue Corvette...an unhappy little car with a wild engine," a 250 hp Chevrolet and a 310 hp Pontiac Bonneville convertible. "Claims made for fuel injection," wrote *MT's* Bill Carroll, "sound like a wallflower's hope chest--lots of hope but not too much chest."

Carroll did hope that F.I. would eventually be improved, perfected, and readily available. The option, unfortunately, was almost too rare to be adequately evaluated. It was even rare on the Corvette.

The fuelies did manage to do rather well during their brief--and suddenly interrupted--racing career. In late 1956, an "independent engineering firm" known as Southern Engineering Development Company (SEDCO) was formed under the direction of Vince Piggins in Atlanta. Says Piggins some 20 years later, "The nucleus of that was through a dealership down there, which fronted it for us--incorporated it, and everything else. We picked up drivers from the NASCAR circuit. We had three running in Grand National, three running in what they called the Convertible Circuit, and three participating in the Short Track Circuits. We also ran three Corvettes out of the shop. I later hired Jim Rathmann to come down and run the show. He had a hot rod

Fireball Roberts takes first at Darlington 500 on Labor Day, 1958, in a 1957 Chevrolet.

shop in Miami, sold parts and raced stock cars. He took the shop over, and that was probably the first time any aggressive team, that is factory team, participated. Chris Economaki referred to it as 'the era of little black cars' because everything we had was black and white and they were easy to paint and fix up. We won practically everything there was to win, taking firsts, seconds and thirds consistently."

In February, 1957, Piggins and manager Rathmann arrived at Daytona with the SEDCO stable of Chevys, loaded for bear. Starting on Tuesday, February 12th, in Class 4 (213 to 259 cid), Chevrolet took the first three places in the official two-way flying mile. (Ford finished fourth, seven seconds off Chevy's winning pace of 102.157 mph). The same day in Class 5 (259 to 305 cid), Chevrolet captured the first 33 out of 37 places, with Paul Goldsmith's best time averaging 131.076. On February 14th, in Big Three competition for automatic transmission four-barrel carburetor engines, Chevrolet took the first three places, best average speed being Al Simonsen's .118.460. The same day in the measured mile standing start acceleration runs, '57 Chevies dominated Class 5, taking the first 18 places-- 19th place went to a Ford, ten seconds later. In Class 4 standing start, 0–60 mph, Chevrolet bowed to Robert Reed's 190 hp Nash Rambler, but six 140 hp *six-cylinder* Chevies finished hot on its tail.

The Pure Oil Manufacturer's Trophy was a Chevy sweep, with a total point count of 574. Ford was a dim second with 309 points, Mercury third at 174. And then, suddenly, what looked like a bright racing future ended.

The same month as Daytona, while Chevrolet ran gallantly on at the Speed Weeks, the Automobile Manufacturers Association met to consider the future of racing participation by auto companies. AMA was meeting in response to urgent representations by the National Safety Council, the American Automobile Association (itself only recently out of racing), and several of its own members who, for various reasons either admirable or corporate, disapproved of the horsepower spiral, racing in general, and advertising derived therefrom. These worthies declared adamantly that contrary to a thousand examples and fifty years of automotive history, racing certainly *did not* improve the breed. A resolution was prepared, for submission to the AMA board of directors, *recommending* (the reader should dwell on that particular word) that members henceforth not participate in racing or competition involving speed of any kind, not encourage the same by outside organizations, refuse to supply "pace cars" in connection with any racing event, and discourage dealers from all similar interests. In April, while this resolution was still in the debate stage, NASCAR helpfully banned fuel injected or supercharged cars in its stock car races. And on June 7th, 1957, the board passed the AMA resolution unanimously.

Some of the events which precipitated the AMA decision, a protective one at best, should be noted. Vince Piggins brought them to the author's attention in the order of their occurrence, following a sweeping parallel investigation of the automobile by the Department of Commerce, the Bureau of Public Roads, and a representative of the House Interstate Highway Safety Subcommittee in June, 1956: (a) A threat by a member of the house committee to place a tax on horsepower on August 31st; (b) a threat by Congress to consider a safe car law September 13th; (c) adoption of a resolution by the New York State Policy Advisory Board to study legislation which might be necessary to curb the horsepower race in advertising on January 15th, 1957.

The wording of the ban should be carefully noted. It was a *recommendation*, not an ironclad ruling. Regard-

"Get out and get under," a phrase taken seriously during the 1957 racing effort by Possum Jones...

less, General Motors led the way by giving its full endorsement to the resolution on May 23, two weeks before it was formally adopted by the AMA. All other members likewise approved and adopted the resolution, but as Piggins noted, "Between 1957 and 1962, there was official but sometimes only token compliance with the resolution, with some industry members unofficially continuing their racing activities." In June, 1962, Ford withdrew its support of the resolution. Chrysler followed Ford, as well as AMC. Meanwhile, GM reaffirmed its stand supporting the resolution. SEDCO was dissolved, and as Piggins told this writer, "Each of the individuals who worked for Southern Engineering went his separate way and continued racing. Jim Rathmann went back to the performance parts business in Miami. In 1961 he took over a Chevrolet-Cadillac dealership in Melbourne, Florida." Walt MacKenzie took a job at Product Information, Vince Piggins joined Product Performance at Chevrolet.

The facts behind the AMA resolution should be carefully qualified. To quote Paul Van Valkenburgh, "This wasn't an outside regulatory body imposing its will on helpless manufacturers. The directors were made up of 15 top executives from all the automotive corporations. However, the decision might be better understood when you realize that included men from Studebaker-Packard, Kaiser Motors, American Motors, International Harvester, Mack Truck, White Motor, and Diamond T. What did they have to lose?"

In a way, GM was grateful. The horsepower race had required an enormous amount of cash, not only in race sponsorship and promotion, but in bare bones engineering development and research.

Above: does girl match car? Bumper-grille combo on '50 Buick.

Left, the 1957 Chevy's distinctive twin lance windsplits.

Extensively modified 1957 dashboard continued to group instruments, position glove box in center, and use warning lights for oil-amps.

Piggins notes, "we kept this parts business alive because there was a demand for it. We had parts in service, there was no point in scrapping them. The resolution said nothing about being able to supply these parts for the individual to do his own thing. The manufacturer couldn't do it, and he couldn't use the advertising that came from racing."

Chevrolet didn't exactly fade into the racing woodwork. At the Southern "500" at Darlington, South Carolina, on

Labor Day weekend, Speedy Thompson lived up to his name, piloting his '57 Chevy home first with an average time of 100.100 mph. Even in 1958, the same race was won by a 1957 Chevy, driven by Fireball Roberts and averaging 102.590 mph. (In 1959 Jim Reed's 1959 Chevy won with an average time of 111.836. Chevrolets were remembered at Darlington for this string of successes, which began in 1955 and was interrupted only once, by Curtis Turner's Ford, in 1956.)

One of the reasons behind Chevy's post-ban success may have been a little booklet of just 23 pages, available through Chevrolet dealers in the Spring of 1957--one of the first "How To" books on racing and performance. Entitled *1957 Chevrolet Stock Car Competition Guide*, it told exactly how to get performance out of the available components and options, and how to win with them. Ostensibly it was prepared for dealers "to assist individuals who plan to participate," and was "not intended to encourage, but rather to inform, the newcomer of techniques that promote greater safety and higher entertainment value for all who enjoy stock car competition in the highest traditions of the sport."

In fact, the *Guide* detailed just about everything anybody needed to make a stormer out of his Chevy: heavy-duty equipment and parts; special modifications for engine, chassis and body; setting up for a track; competition tuning; spare parts and equipment; even data on registration, complete with addresses. And it was in circulation long after the AMA decided that racing was hazardous to our health.

One can look back now, with the added appreciation of hindsight, on the effects of the self-imposed racing resolution. Within five years, full-size American cars were by and large heavier, clumsier, more dangerous, more unproven than they'd been in years, and if it wasn't for the advent of the compacts, with all their potential in handling and performance, the Detroit scene might have been dim indeed for decades to come.

Even then, most observers qualified to comment could see the writing on the wall. Tom McCahill was one of them. "This was the straw that got the camel's belly back on the ground again," Uncle Tom said. "When an ad man can't write about his product's success at Pikes Peak, Daytona Beach or Darlington, or how fast it gets away from a traffic light, what's he got left? All he can do is tell about the hand-woven Indian rugs on the floor, the Da-Vinci sculptured door handles, or the 'ten miles per gallon' it averaged under the featherfoot of a professional economy jockey.

"The bare truth is that, as a crop, the 1959 cars are less safe than they were two years ago, because many of them have gone back to that ten year old pitch of trying to build for Madame Ceil Shapiro of the Bronx the featheriest ride on Featherbed Lane. Some cars look to me as though their engineers had lost all heart in their products."

The 1957 Chevrolet--the last, as far as we can see, eminently collectable full-size Chevrolet automobile--was a nice way to end a three-year era of superlative accomplishments in design, engineering and competition. It was an interesting combination--a facelifted 1955 body, coupled with engineering advances almost overwhelming in their complexity. Granted, Plymouth (actually all Chrysler products) had overtaken it as *Motor Trend's* "best-handling car," and the all-new Ford was cleverly priced just a few dollars below each corresponding Chevy, and the overall appearance of the thing wasn't quite as simple and elegant as it had been when it first hit the American scene, two years before. But in some ways, it was a better car. *Motor Life*, perhaps, best summed up the '57 when it wrote: "The car has been extensively restyled to bring it up to date. And it's still short of the 'new look.' On the other side, it has outstanding quality and exceptional performance--and these are long-term values. Maybe the compromise is the happy combination buyers want. If so, Chevrolet will prove it this year." It did. And it still does today.

A lot of people would remember the 1955-57 Chevrolet. Indeed, almost five million of the cars were produced-- just about everybody had one once! But for them, the excitement would be over in 1958, as the Division produced an entirely different car, the beginning of a completely different design direction.

There is one other thing to say about the era of the "Hot One." This subject doesn't amount to the proverbial hill of beans production-wise (23,000 units out of 4.8 million), but it is remembered today as one of the most interesting station wagons ever created, a Motorama idea, that actually went into limited production. We speak, of course, of that unforgettable styling achievement, the Chevrolet Nomad "hardtop" station wagon.

Rare Nomad clay from GM Photographic shows project under way after enthusiastic reception to Corvette Nomad in 1954 Motorama.

CHAPTER FIVE

Chevy Nomad: Queen of the Line

Starting in 1949, two major design thrusts occupied the thoughts of automotive stylists: pillarless styling and passenger-car-like station wagons. The 1955-57 Chevrolet Nomad was a strikingly handsome combination of both these concepts and, given their simultaneous increase in popularity, appeared to many at the time a sure winner. Like most great cars, however, it had a long list of varied antecedents.

The origin of the station wagon, somewhere between the early Cantrell-bodied "depot hacks" on Model T Ford chassis and 1923 Star--was long forgotten by the late Forties, when the Detroit manufacturers began to take a fresh look at high-volume people haulers. Chevrolet's own station wagon predecessors were crude vehicles, scarcely more than covered trucks, and very far removed from the neat, clean, all-steel wagons fostered by Willys-Overland in 1946 and Plymouth in 1949. The reason why Chevrolet, Plymouth and the rest got busy on new wagon ideas when they did is succinctly explained by statistics: in 1940 only one out of 100 cars was a station wagon; by 1948, the per-

centage was 2.8; by 1957, it had risen to 15. America's population was on the move after World War II--from urban to suburban areas, from farms to cities, from job to job. Detroit, as usual, simply saw a need and filled it.

The pillarless coupe or "hardtop convertible" as it was first known originated immediately after the war, when Chrysler built a handful of its wood-embellished Town & Country convertibles with a permanent steel top pirated from a business coupe. In 1949, Kaiser introduced the Virginian, which it called a "four-door hardtop" but which was in reality a sedan without "B" pillars--and all side window frames on the Virginian were fixed, remaining in place when the glass was rolled down. So the first genuine production hardtops were really built by General Motors, in the form of the 1949 Buick Roadmaster Riviera, Oldsmobile 98 Holiday, and Cadillac Series 62 Coupe de Ville.

From these beginnings, the hardtop craze rocketed to a point where it held over one-fifth of the market by 1956. By then, two-door models were industry-wide, and many companies had four-door versions as well. Combine market

Oldsmobile's 1946 76 wagon was typical of traditional designs.

By 1949 the Olds 76 wagon had changed very dramatically.

First wagon with all-steel body was Willys-Overland's, 1946.

K-F pioneered sedan-wagons; 1951 Frazer is illustrated here.

In 1949, Plymouth produced first passenger-car steel wagon.

Willys planned, but did not build, hardtop wagon for 1955.

percentages for the hardtop and wagon, and one can understand why many in the industry thought the combination of both styles a good idea.

Chevrolet wasn't the only company playing with this idea by 1955. Willys had planned a two-door hardtop wagon in its Aero passenger car line for that year, but recurrent losses and the exit of Kaiser-Willys from passenger car manufacture prevented it from appearing. Chrysler displayed an experimental wagon, the "Plainsman," in 1956--its fabric-padded metal roof was stepped and cantilevered, and its windowline was definitely hardtop-inspired. Rambler actually built a production four-door hardtop in its Cross Country line for 1956, copping a "first" that is all but forgotten today. And Chevrolet built the 1955-57 Nomad--a model that, historically speaking, is the diametric opposite of the Cross Country. A true hardtop it wasn't--the "B" pillar is too thick and doesn't retract--but over 5000 people own, drive or restore Chevy Nomads today. One would be hard-pressed to find a dozen Cross Country collectors.

Good styling, functional design, and historical significance are not, however, always accompanied by public acceptance. At the time the Nomad did not enjoy great popularity. Its 1955 sales were underwhelming; they diminished in 1956, and again in 1957, the true Nomad's last year. But the car succeeded in less tangible ways, harbinger of a new generation of stylish, luxurious station wagons, ringing down the final curtain for the truck-like carry-alls built sans finesse from time immemorial. Thus, the Nomad is remembered by today's enthusiasts: an historic watershed, but above all a very pretty car, possibly the most aesthetically beautiful wagon every produced.

Like all things GM in those days, Nomad styling began with Harley Earl. It started where many progressive designs started, as a dream car based on the 1953 Corvette.

In 1946 Chrysler built seven Town & Country two-door hardtops.

Kaiser Virginian, 1949, was almost, but not quite pillarless.

The 1949 Cadillac Coupe de Ville was true pillarless hardtop.

Rambler Cross Country four-door hardtop-wagon. *Chrysler's experimental Plainsman, from 1956.* *Plymouth's Cabana show wagon appeared in 1958*

Appearing in the Motorama of that year, the fiberglass 'Vette was aimed at young people, and they received it enthusiastically. The lithe sports roadster duly became the first GM dream car to go into production substantially unaltered--and just five months after the Motorama. As preparations were made for the 1954 Motorama, Clare MacKichan and company began thinking of what they might do for a Corvette encore. "The Corvette theme was a popular one," he recalls, "and thus when ideas for 1954 Motorama 'dream cars' were being considered, it figured prominently in the Chevrolet area." What became the Nomad was begun at this point: a station wagon version of the Chevy Corvette. "As far as we can recall," adds MacKichan, "Mr. Earl should get the credit for suggesting it.

"The Chevrolet studio in 1954, unlike that of a year earlier, was deeply involved in the dream car project. Mr. Earl brought ideas in from many other areas. A young man named Carl Renner, who was working in a special studio, had come up with a sketch for a station wagon roof that caught Earl's eye. Bringing this idea to the Chevrolet studio, Earl asked that it be incorporated into a station wagon version, as one of the Corvette idea cars at the 1954 Motorama. As it turned out, a production open Corvette, a hardtop Corvette, a fastback Corvair [combining the

words "Corvette" and "Bel Air"] and a Corvette Nomad sport station wagon* were shown."

Originally, Harley Earl had some elaborate plans for the Nomad roof which never got beyond the conceptual stage: the stainless steel rear portion would telescope, forming an opening. This never appeared on the Corvette Nomad, but it did influence the final design, as the roof exterior had nine grooves in it and the interior headliner was distinguished with corresponding horizontal chrome bows, a carry through of Earl's idea.

Said MacKichan, "We talked about that idea. We talked about a lot of things. We always do on our cars. Some are not as practical as others, and that was one that wasn't quite as practical as it might have been--a 'collapsible cup' roof really isn't too grand when you consider the possibility of leakage. Of course, we then would have had a cantilever situation with no support in the back and that was another small problem. When Chevrolet management was approached with the idea of a stainless steel roof which telescoped, our idea was discarded rather quickly,

---

* This car is called the "Waldorf Nomad," since it premiered at the Motorar ld at the Waldorf Astoria in New York City. For simplification accuracy, it will be referred to herewith as the "Corvette Nomad," though the colloquialism is acceptable.

The Corvette or Waldorf Nomad show car from 1954. Carl Renner artwork, below left to right: hardtop with much glass and thin pillars (early 1950s); ditto with flying wing roof (1957); same idea again with Delta theme in hood, and cantilever-type rear quarter.

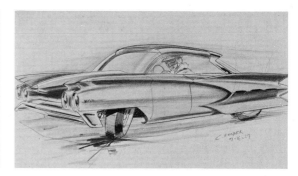

Cadillac Park Avenue show car used brushed stainless steel roof.

because of lack of practicality. So we simulated it, with the grooved effect."

Carl Renner recalls: "Mr. Earl always favored stainless steel brushed panels--it was one of his favorite materials at that time, though it would have been too costly. He always went all the way--and then backed off." [The brushed aluminum roof did appear in the 1954 Motorama on the Cadillac Park Avenue; in the 1955 Motorama on the first Eldorado Brougham "dream car," and in December, 1956, at the New York Automobile Show as the production Eldorado Brougham.]

Harley Earl summed up the roof treatment that finally evolved on the Corvette Nomad, in *The Saturday Evening Post* later in 1954: "Just a few months ago I was reminded again of the long way automobile design has come and the fact that there is no end to it. I was observing the [Corvette] Nomad station wagon in the 1954 Motorama, and it was clear that my long-time effort to lower American automobiles had indeed succeeded. I was looking right across the top of the Nomad's roof. And there was visible evidence that every accomplishment can raise a new problem. To an average man, the Nomad's roof was now vis-

ible as a part of the car's conformation. So, for perhaps the first time in automobile history, we had had to give this unbroken roof expanse a decorative treatment. We grooved it. I hope designing is always like that."

For the Motorama, the Corvette Nomad fiberglass body was mounted on a 1953 Chevrolet station wagon chassis. Appearances at the front and rear were Corvette-inspired. The sporty wagon roof line was Carl Renner's, along with the distinctive wide-slanted "B" pillar. The latter's angle corresponded with the thin slanted rear "C" pillar, which eliminated blind spots and was flanked by curved rear quarter glass wrapping around to the sloping rear profile, which also contributed to better vision. (In the show car the rear glass dropped into the tailgate; this feature was not "production" on Chevy wagons until 1959.)

The decorations worn on the tailgate--"bananas," "graphics" or chrome strips, depending on who describes them--were designed by Chuck Stebbins who was in charge of the body design studio. They were destined to become the hallmark of the Nomad. On the Corvette Nomad, tailgate hinges were 3½ inches below the bottom of the gate in the rear pan, and developed as two main ribs traveling up the tailgate, flanked by an additional five ribs.

Which came first, the hinges or the ribs? Carl Renner feels that development went something like this: "Looking at that as a designer, with the chrome strips going all the way underneath, it was apparently decided that they should run through since there was no full bumper on the Corvette Nomad. It did give a little bit of protection in the area between the side rear fender bumpers and the little frame around the license plate. There are many possible reasons why it may have been done: perhaps to camouflage a hinge, or just because of the carry through of an idea or theme. Many designers played with these ribs or rub rails. Chuck Stebbins put them on all types of cars--coupes, sedans--they dressed up a car. If you will note,

All photographs on this page are of late prototype Nomads from the GM Styling Section. Differences from production models include the seat trim, support attachment and back-up lights. Top car uses the Corvette Nomad seat support and has a temporary window slider. Missing items include weatherstripping, window latch, shock plates, tailgate inspection plate, bumper bolts and striker guide.

160

A 1955 Nomad with optional body sill trim and fender guards.

Another fine '55 shows special eyebrow trim and molding.

From GM Photographic, the production Bel Air Nomad of 1955.

Nomad "B" pillar was inspired by L'Universelle van--or, in the case of these renderings, the "Expedier." One such van was built.

1955 STATION WAGON DIMENSIONS (IN INCHES)

	Wheelbase	Overall length	Passengers	Height, tail-gate opening	Height, cargo space	Length, cargo space, seat folded	Length, cargo space, seat up	Length, cargo space, tailgate open
Chevrolet								
Four Door	115	197.1	6	31	47	84	47	106
Nomad	115	197.1	6	31	45	86	43	109
Ford								
Ranch Wagon	115.5	198	6	32	37	76	45	98
Country Sedan	115.5	198	6/8	33	37	84	48	106
Plymouth								
Belvedere and Plaza	115	208.6	6/8	33	38	81	48	104

Elegance was the background theme as the 1955 Nomad debuted.

right and left of the license plate housing the chrome bumper strips do line up visually with the tailgate strips."

The reason for the appearance of seven distinctive tailgate strips (with the center one incorporating handle and lock) was basically a decorative one. The idea may have originated from the chrome slide rails which were often put on backs of vehicles or on floors, so steamer trunks would slide readily without scratching the floor.

The Corvette Nomad was not a running vehicle, though it could have been, "if Chevrolet had been willing to spend the money for the conversion," as MacKichan stated. The name Nomad, which originated at the 1954 Motorama, "was wrapped up in connotations of a wanderlust, gypsy-like freedom, all things that the thoughts of a sports wagon conjured up. Many of us wanted to see the Nomad go into production as a wagon version of the Corvette, but the early Corvette calendar year sales were not too promising [1953: 183; 1954: 2780; 1955: 1639] and as a consequence the decision was made to produce the wagon as a standard size Chevrolet for the 1955 model year." At this time, the question arose with regard to continuing the Corvette, itself.

Carl Renner mentions that "the name Nomad came from the studio, which is the way things evolved in those days." MacKichan later recalled: "I remember, I pushed that."

Originally, the Corvette Nomad was finished in white fiberglass, but for the Motorama the lower body was painted blue (Earl's favorite color), so the white roof and slanted "B" pillar would contrast. Both Renner and MacKichan insist only *one* Corvette Nomad was created--and it is gone forever. Says MacKichan, "To the best of our knowledge, the original Corvette Nomad was scrapped sometime in the 1960s and no longer exists. Persistent stories crop up from time to time that we have it squirreled away in a warehouse somewhere in Detroit, but unfortunately this seems to be a myth."

When the Corvette Nomad appeared at the 1954 Motorama, it was reported that crowds raved over its styling. MacKichan puts it this way: "They were enthusiastic... but I don't think that's what really got to Harley Earl. The friends he associated with were so enthusiastic that he told his manager, Howard O'Leary, to get me on the phone. He said, 'When I get back in two days I want to see that whole car, and how you would do it on a '55 Chevrolet.'"

Work began immediately. When the author commented, "That must have been *some* job, in such a little amount of time," MacKichan replied, "Oh, yes, but that was fun

Rare Nomad ad ran in Resort Management, *April 1955 edition.*

Pontiac liked Nomad, borrowed design despite Chevy's reluctance. Left, the 1955 Pontiac Safari. Above, the 1956 variation.

because we liked the car so much. Just the idea of getting it into production made it really worthwhile."

Renner was set to work--with scissors in hand. Mac-Kichan remembers that "the Nomad roof was taken from a full size drawing, cut apart, stretched out and mated to the basic design of the 1955 Chevrolet lower body, windshield, etc., which was done in the body design studio. The innovations of the Corvette Nomad were carried into the production car, introduced in February, 1955. The hardtop front door glass framing, forward sloping rear quarters, the wide "B" pillar, the fluted roof, the wrap-around rear side glass, the rear wheel housing cut-out, and the seven vertical accent strips on the tailgate, were all retained in a remarkably good translation from the dream car."

Carl Renner recalls the process of adjusting the show car to the '55 production body: "It went quite fast, taking that roof and adapting it, jockeying around to match the production version, step by step. But there again [we had] good leadership and good decisions. We went ahead."

As the 1955 Chevrolet Nomad evolved out of the 1954 Motorama Corvette Nomad, so did a similar wagon for Pontiac: the 1955 Safari. Though not the subject of this chapter, a very brief examination of the Safari is in order.

Its production numbers were less than half that of the Chevrolet Nomad (3760 in 1955, 4042 in 1956, 1292 in 1957, totalling 9094). In 1957, the Pontiac Star Chief Custom Safari was the two-door hardtop styled version. Pontiac made three other station wagons in the 1957 Safari series. a two- and four-door Chieftain, and a four-door Super Chief, none of which incorporated the Nomad roof styling.

Pontiac's Safari was on a 122-inch wheelbase, compared to Chevrolet's 115 inches. Its front wheels were five inches farther forward than the Nomad's; its rear wheels were two inches farther back. Doors, roof, glass, tailgate, inside garnish moldings from the 1955, 1956 and 1957 version were respectively interchangeable with Chevrolet Nomads.

Renner explained the Safari's birth in this manner: "It was a chance for Pontiac to have something new by adapting the Nomad upper to their lower. I think when Pontiac saw it, they felt they could do something with it. At that time, I recall, Chevrolet didn't like the idea. Chevy always wanted things exclusive. Management wanted it for the Pontiac line--so it worked out."

Since work did not begin on the 1955 Chevrolet Nomad

until January 1954, one can readily understand why it couldn't appear at the October new car introduction. At the January 1955 Motorama both the 1955 Chevrolet Nomad and the 1955 Pontiac Safari debuted at the Waldorf Astoria in New York City. GM moved fast.

Approximately 300 semi-hand-built Nomads were assembled to appear at dealerships and shows in very early 1955. Though it cannot be proven now, many feel these cars had two distinguishing characteristics: the handle on the center tailgate strip and the outside reveal molding around the rear quarter windows. The tailgate handle was nicknamed the "knuckle-buster": You stood a good chance of doing exactly that every time you used it. Wayne Oakley, technical editor of the National Nomad Club's *Nomad News*, has noted that this particular item was used on many more Nomads than the first 300: "Having done a little research on the subject, it appears to me that the change to a different handle was made somewhere around body number 4000 in 1955 Nomad production." As for the moldings, Wayne informed the author that they were something "other than stainless steel, as found on later '55 Nomads. They appeared to be a stamped metal that had been chromed, because a magnet would cling to them."

How did the 1955 Nomad differ from production '55s? In a nutshell, its body shared very little sheet metal with the rest of the line from the cowl back, while engines, transmissions, chassis, frame and running gear were identical with other 1955 production.

As Clare MacKichan mentioned previously, the styling features translated from the Corvette Nomad were the most obvious ones. The Nomad hood and front fenders were 1955 production, as were the grille and front bumper. The dash was identical to that of the 1955 Bel Air. Doors were hardtop styled, but differed slightly from the hardtop configuration as the Nomad had no beltline dip. The windshield and ventilator glass were interchangeable with that of a hardtop or convertible. The rest of the side glass, as well as the liftgate glass differed. The floor was shared with a two-door station wagon. Quarter panels differed because of rear wheel housing dimensions as well as the straight beltline. Tail- and liftgates differed from the 1955 station wagon line. The liftgate was a heavy die-cast metal frame, chrome plated. The tailgate had seven chrome strips attached. The identifying Nomad script appeared near the tailgate upper edge, above the center chrome strip, for all three years. The entire rear profile was slanted more than the regular station wagon line and the tailgate cables and liftgate hold-up struts were longer on the Nomad. The roofline and "B" and "C" pillars were, of course, distinctive to the Nomad line.

Outside, the 1955 Nomad wore no rear quarter panel molding trim as appeared on the rest of the Bel Air series, and the Chevrolet emblem and Bel Air script were moved to the rear fender area beyond the gas tank filler door. Taillamps were stock 1955, and the rear bumper was identical with other '55 wagons. Inside, linoleum covered the

The Motorama Nomad show car, displayed in January, 1955.

rear deck area as in other wagons. The headliner was vinyl, decorated with chrome bows--which also dressed the Bel Air hardtop series, but differed in dimension.

The 1955 Chevrolet Nomad had three additional characteristics which further enhanced its originality : chrome headlamp and front fender/door trim, a special interior, and a rear wheel cutout. These six pieces of decorative white metal are often referred to as "eyebrows" and side trim. They were designed by Bob Veryzer, who explained them as an individual treatment to enhance the Nomad versus the regular '55 line. The insert formed within the side trim was painted white, a treatment similar to the rear side molding on the Bel Air series.

An all vinyl "waffle and ribbed" interior appeared on Nomad seats. Door and side panels carried an attractive combination of plain and waffle vinyl trim, and interior

The "knuckle buster," from early Nomad production.

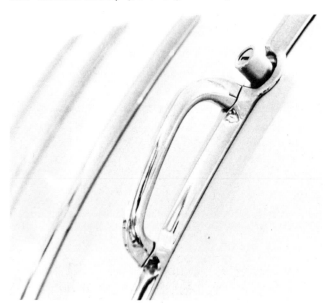

wheel housings were covered with plain vinyl. Interestingly, the 1955 Nomad interior treatment was quite similar to that of the 1956 and 1957 Corvette, which incorporated the waffle pattern. Ed Donaldson was involved in interiors at this time, and was remembered as the individual most responsible for the attractive, durable treatment.

The outside rear fender contour differed somewhat from regular 1955 production, showing a high rear wheel housing cutout--a direct carryover from the Corvette Nomad. It lent a feeling of lightness to the sheet metal, and was particularly necessitated by the Nomad's rather high, straight beltline.

After 1955, Nomads did not have these three unique characteristics. The distinctive exterior side molding was dropped; they shared interiors with the Bel Air line, rear sheet metal was as in regular production. Making these three concessions to standardization was an attempt to reduce the Nomad's high production costs, further magnified by its low sales. By the time the Division began tooling up for 1956, even the continuance of the Nomad was in some doubt.

The car's disappointing sales (8530 in 1955) were not aided by the press coverage, which of course came much later than most 1955 models. But late or not, the comment was generally good. "The Detroit pendulum is swinging back to variety," said Don MacDonald of *Motor Trend*, "[through] demand from the same public that killed variety through lack of interest in the Thirties...Ponderous GM senses it, or you wouldn't have the Nomad, the Safari, or Rambler with its Cross-Country." (How MacDonald figured GM to be responsible for the Cross Country he unfortunately didn't say.) *Motor Trend* ended by describing the Nomad as "the longed for styling wedding between the production sports car and the family workhorse." Later in the year, the magazine gave it third place

Above: Two-tone paint enhanced 1956 Nomad.

Below left to right: Reversal of quarter molding angle, 1956 hood bird, "Vees" particular to 1956 Nomad and Nomad script on tailgate.

in their "most aesthetically styled" contest for '55, behind the Chrysler 300 and Ford Thunderbird. The editors called it "compact, clean, utilitarian, a successful combination of form and function. It has an elegance that you don't often see in a small car...not something left over from the classic era, but a real 1955 elegance..."

Being an exceptional design in the first place, the Nomad translated quite easily into its facelifted 1956 and 1957 forms. The two-toning spear of 1956 wore well; though lacking the simplicity of 1955, the '56's lines remained attractive and not too gaudy.

A few characteristics of the 1956 edition were particular to that year. The angle of the vertical quarter molding trim, separating the two-tone treatment, was reversed--so that it corresponded with the angle of the slanted "B" pillar. Bill Steere, who came up with 1956's two-toning, is credited with this trim change. The 1956 also displayed chrome "vees" beneath the taillights on V-8 models, but these were not interchangeable with the 1955 variety owing to different sheet metal. The 1956 "vees" were unique--other models signified the V-8 with a single large "V" device on trunk or tailgate. Finally, 1956 seat-insert material on the Nomad was interchangeable with 1956 Bel

As stock as they come: 1957 owned by Bob Lang, Rochester, NY.

Air two- and four-door hardtops and the Beauville wagon.

For the second year in a row, *Motor Trend* selected Nomad as one of the year's most beautiful cars, though with some qualifications: "Its distinct personal-car feel forces certain features that must limit its usefulness: the low roofline, compact overall package, sharply sloping rear. More unified than the overdecorated Pontiac Safari." But production dropped by over 400 units (to 8103), despite the advantage of a full year's marketing--the '56 Nomad had come in with the rest of the line in November 1955.

The Nomad took equally well to the 1957 facelift, though the handwriting was assuredly on the wall by then and its future was limited. Trim became more standardized: interiors were shared with the Bel Air line. There was no special exterior trim other than the Nomad script and small gold "V" on the tailgates of V-8 powered models, and rear wheel cut-outs were stock '57. But the handsome hardtop styling blended gracefully with the '57 facelift, complimenting the massive front bumper/grille and finned rear fenders with their aluminum inserts.

"Behold the Beauty Queen of all Station Wagons!" said Chevy ads as the '57 Nomad debuted. It was a far cry from the light and delicate Corvette Nomad of 1954--but the heritage was there. As a show car, Chevy said with truth, "it thrilled millions, and its special beauty will win *you* over the moment you set eyes on it." It may have--but it would be for the last time.

Only 6534 1957 Chevrolet Nomads came off the line--a 2000 car drop from 1955 and 1500 less than 1956. Total Nomad production for the three years was therefore 23,167--only .48 percent of Chevy's total 1955-57 wagon production of over half a million. In terms of numbers, the Nomad strictly didn't matter.

"The wagon with the sports car flair...that much prefers carrying golf clubs to gardening tools," would prefer such dalliance no more, for in 1958 the name "Nomad" was applied to the workaday line of four-door wagons, as it would be through 1961. Again in 1968, the name was revived for the bottom-line Chevelle, where it remained through 1972. Finally, in 1973, Chevrolet laid the by-then overworked name of Nomad to rest. It was a long time coming.

Like the regular line, the 1955 Nomad was the best of the three years, because its styling was pure, incorporated on the 1955 body from the drawing board. "Consumer reticence about the 'Ferrari' grille caused a return to the full width grille for 1956," notes Clare MacKichan, "and this, plus two-tone color carried into the body sides, detracted from the purity of the original Nomad theme. Corporate management was looking for flashier cars and the 1957 version of the Nomad was even less pure. But the distinctive Nomad design carried through nonetheless."

The designers like MacKichan naturally regretted their baby's demise. "It was a very sad day when they decided not to build the car [for 1958] as far as we were concerned," MacKichan says. "And for lack of sales! Little did we--or little did they--realize how popular the car would become. Of course a lot of the popularity is because of the few numbers. If you had two million of them on the road, they wouldn't [now] be quite as popular."

Two million--two thousand--two hundred--it probably doesn't matter very much. The Chevrolet Nomad looked good then; it still looks good today. Its styling is timeless --and memorable. As MacKichan said in 1972, while addressing a National Nomad Club convention, "It is a great satisfaction to observe that the current growing popularity of sports wagons was predicted by the designers at GM styling some 20 years before the public was ready..."

Hindsight, as Churchill said, has one major problem: it's always made after the fact. But it's valuable in analyzing

They called it a Nomad, but the 1958 job was something else.

the reasons for the Nomad's demise. Primarily, the car was expensive--with the largest price tag of any regular Chevrolet passenger car--$2571 was the V-8 Nomad's tag, $200 more than the four-door Bel Air wagon and $265 more than the convertible. Even the Corvette was only $360 more than the Nomad in 1955.

The price was rough enough--but then it only bought *two doors*. And that was Nomad problem number two. Standard-sized, two-door wagons never have attracted many buyers. Still, some of the rumors about Nomad's lack of cargo space are unfounded, as witness charts in these pages, and its 1955 interior was a practical all-vinyl one that was useful as it was attractive. Its greenhouse design provided unheard-of visibility for the middle-Fifties, although subsequent surveys of buyer habits at that time indicate that this safety advantage was in fact a marketing albatross. A Nomad can get pretty hot on a sunny day, and air circulation wasn't the best through sliding windows,

170

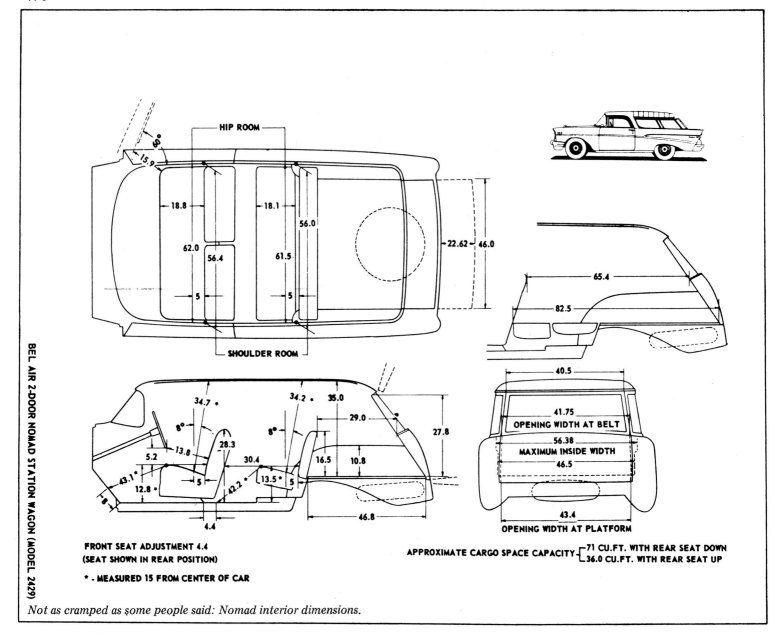

HIP ROOM

18.8   18.1

56.0

62.0
56.4   61.5

5   5

SHOULDER ROOM

22.62 46.0

65.4

82.5

34.7 *   34.2 * 35.0
8°   8° 29.0
13.8   28.3   27.8
5.2   30.4
43.1 *   16.5 10.8
12.8   42.2 * 13.5 * 5
4.4   46.8

40.5

41.75
OPENING WIDTH AT BELT
56.38
MAXIMUM INSIDE WIDTH
46.5

43.4
OPENING WIDTH AT PLATFORM

FRONT SEAT ADJUSTMENT 4.4
(SEAT SHOWN IN REAR POSITION)

* - MEASURED 15 FROM CENTER OF CAR

APPROXIMATE CARGO SPACE CAPACITY ⌈71 CU.FT. WITH REAR SEAT DOWN
⌊36.0 CU.FT. WITH REAR SEAT UP

BEL AIR 2-DOOR NOMAD STATION WAGON (MODEL 2429)

Not as cramped as some people said: Nomad interior dimensions.

and factory air at $565 was prohibitively expensive and not nearly as efficient as it is today.

There were other problems, indicating less than adequate production engineering. Traveling for long with the liftgate open would not only subject occupants to exhaust fumes, but could actually warp the liftgate. Rain leaks

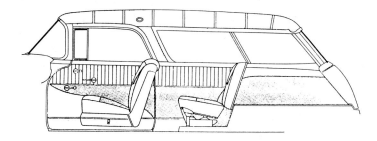

Chevrolet diagram showing Nomad interior trim configuration with sporty yet practical vinyl door panels and headliner.

were common to all Nomads, and the liftgate rain gutter would have done better had it been placed on the trailing edge of the roof. "I guess you would have to label [the liftgate] a poor engineering job." comments Clare MacKichan. "We designers are not responsible for everything. We'd like to dump that on somebody else."

Frankly, it was fortunate that the Nomad roofline didn't continue. (The only two-door wagon in 1958 was the plain-Jane Yeoman.) The design was compatible with, and designed for, the 1955-57 models, and would not have enhanced 1958 styling, or vice-versa. As for 1959, the thought of a hardtop-wagon of that vintage is painful. The end of the true Nomad was appropriate in 1957.

The idea of hardtop-wagons, kicked off by the Nomad, did not end in 1957, however. The year before, American Motors' Rambler had built a four-door hardtop wagon, and

in '57 GM's Buick Caballero and Oldsmobile Fiesta were wagon bodies with pillarless four-door configuration. Ford built a two-door hardtop wagon with its 1957 Mercury, and a show model Plymouth called the Cabana featured four-door hardtop wagon styling in 1958. The GM and Ford production versions quit after 1959, but Chrysler filled the gap in 1960 with its Town & Country four-door hardtop wagons in both Windsor and New Yorker series.

Chrome decorated tailgate enhanced by good-looking 1955 design.

Last of the true Nomads, the 1957 was almost as purely beautiful as the original article, thanks to careful blending of lines.

Joined by Dodge, these were sold through 1964.

The whole phenomenon, from Nomad to Town & Country, may be summed up by the trite but ofttimes appropriate saying, "It seemed like a good idea at the time." Considering that 36 percent of the automotive market was given over to hardtops and wagons during 1956-57, it was a very good idea. But like many compromises, it melded the vulgarisms of two different things without retaining the virtues. Those big, garish four-door hardtops of Buick and Olds became even uglier--if that was possible--by the addition of a station wagon rear end. It was like putting a bustle on a lady wrestler.

At the same time one must judge the advent of hardtop-wagons as a necessary part of automotive development. Though not entirely workable, and fortunately not eternal, they stimulated many features that are today judged advantageous. During the Fifties, the nation experienced tremendous growth and movement, shifting not only houses but places of employment, industry and commerce. The station wagon played a big role here, and though it no longer commands as high a percentage of the market, it is still an important part of our way of life. It may get smaller--it *should* get smaller--but it will probably never disappear. "Where the perambulator rolleth and the power mower hummeth," wrote Devon Francis, "the station wagon cometh."

While the "Queen of the Line" for 1955-57 did not succeed in the marketplace, it surely was a success in dispensing influence--and maybe as far as individual models are concerned, that's what it's all about. Undoubtedly it was a remarkable car, perhaps the only station wagon in automotive history to receive such plaudits for style and flair.

Imaginative photography depicts major changes in rear-end treatment which developed for 1958.

CHAPTER SIX

New Eras, New Challenges

In 1957, according to some statistics anyway, Ford passenger car production caught and passed Chevrolet--for the first time since 1935. In 1958, Chevy came back with a brand new design, more powerful engines, all-coil spring suspension, and an air ride suspension option, and handily outsold Ford by a quarter million units. It also gleaned 30 percent of the passenger car market for the first time in its history.

All of this might suggest to the casual observer that Chevrolet offered a vastly improved product in 1958. Not necessarily so. The cars suited Fifties vernacular by being longer, lower, wider and heavier on average than their predecessors. But in the judgement of time--the only arbiter of a car's ultimate impact *as a car*--the 1958 Chevrolet was less successful. Few are sought after by today's collectors. The Hot One of 1955-57, meanwhile, is possibly the most popular standard passenger car of the whole postwar era among today's restorers.

To achieve such credibility 20 or more years removed from its birth, the Hot One needed more than simple popularity. While there's a case for its current desirability in the nostalgia trips of people who remember it when new ("Everybody had one once"), such reasoning doesn't explain why these three years out of all postwar production so captivate today's enthusiasts. There are more factors involved than that. Perhaps they include the relatively clean, unhampered, lithe styling of the cars, particularly the '55; perhaps they involve the advent of Chevy's first performance engines and other mechanical options; perhaps they are based on the dramatic Nomad, or the beautiful Bel Air hardtop of 1955, or the imaginative four-door hardtop of 1956, of the clean convertible of 1957--outstanding models all, whether by comparison with their GM peers or their rivals from other corporations. Probably their popularity stems from all these reasons.

Uncle Tom McCahill, who always said what most enthusiastic drivers wanted to hear, had some telling comments on the longer, heavier, more rounded, less chiseled 1958s shortly after driving them in late 1957. "In this year of de-emphasized performance," he wrote, *"dig, drag, high*

Signifying a coming age of bulkier GM cars with sway-back beltlines was Oldsmobile's Delta show car, a two-door hardtop for 1956.

speed and *acceleration* are considered unprintable words around Detroit, by unanimous agreement of all members of the Automobile Manufacturers Association...It is still possible to buy the Traveling Man's Special with three two-barrel carburetors and a slightly lively cam, or with fuel injection, coupled with its 283 cubic inch engine. There is not much zip-up material available for the bigger [and new for 1958] 348-cubic-inch mill, however.

"One of the questions I asked several of the engineers at Chevrolet was, 'If your name was Joe Zilchdrag and you wanted a heap for unwinding white-hot at Daytona Beach next February, which engine-car combination would it be?' As things stood when I asked the question, it was generally conceded by the boys that more performance could be wrung out of the smaller engine because of valve timing and available equipment." This was an unlikely state of affairs even in 1958, where the public if not the AMA was still interested in performance, and the ever-larger engines

The 1958 Impala sport coupe and Corvette (bottom two cars) traced design heritage to Biscayne and SS show machines.

Most expensive passenger car in the '58 line was the Bel Air Impala convertible, which started at $2841 and weighed 3508 pounds.

The radical "gull wing" rear fenders of the coming 1959s had their beginnings in the slightly concave stern quarters of the 1958s.

they could feed with 25 cent-per-gallon gasoline. Though the 280 bhp 1958 Chevrolet was demonstrably quicker than the 270 bhp 1957, the extremes of performance through factory options were either unavailable or not spoken of.

Instead of performance Chevrolet pushed its restyle--versus mild facelifts for both Ford and Plymouth--plus an unprecedented degree of automotive luxury. Addressing the latter, the Impala was introduced at the top of the Bel Air series--a big car, richly furnished, weighing 3600 pounds and built on a brand new X-type frame. There was a full line of Bel Airs in addition to the Impala, while the former Two-Ten was now called Biscayne and the former One-Fifty was Delray. (Beaches in Florida were popular with model namers this year, though it is perhaps significant that no Chevy bore the name Daytona.)

The state of the opposition was surprisingly good, despite their lack of all-new styling. Ford had a new unit

The '58 design was dropped after just one year because of body sharing at GM. Below, a comparison of rear windows reveals changes.

Late proposal for 1959 shows customizer's grille, hub caps.

body, and a larger 352 cubic inch V-8 with over 300 horse-power; Plymouth retained its outstanding Exner lines of 1957 but its new Golden Commando V-8 engine developed as much as 305 horsepower, and one road test showed it sprinting 0-60 in 7.7 seconds and the quarter mile in 16.1. Chevy's equivalent times with the 280 hp 348 inch engine were 9.1 and 16.5 seconds respectively.

On the surface, the '58 Plymouth and Ford stood to lose sales among buyers for whom restyles were preferable to facelifts, and to gain on Chevy among those who wanted performance. But another factor intervened in the form of the American economy. A recession set in during late 1957, and the industry built only four and one-quarter million cars for 1958, against six million plus in 1957. When the scores were added up, Chevy had its aforementioned 30 percent slice on 275,000 less cars; Ford was down a whopping 700,000 units, from 25.6 to 22.3 percent of the market. Plymouth tailed off 250,000 cars, and from 10.6 to 9.6 percent, maintaining a tenuous hold on third place.

In retrospect, therefore, the 1958 Chevrolet is considered by many as the car that helped save GM in a quite disastrous year. At the time, says Carl Renner, "many people thought the design was good, however there were those that referred to the rear fenders as World War I barrage balloons, due to their shape and fullness. It was the first suggestion of a concave fin, leading into the larger fins in 1959." So the 1958 could be summarized as a successful car for the time. If not of historic dimension, it came through with a brand new design in the precise year when sales would be hardest to get--which was of import to Chevrolet, as well as to major rivals subsisting on facelifts.

Considering its relatively good record, then, it was a surprise to many that the 1958 design was killed after just one year, replaced by a new, radical finned affair for 1959. Though it doesn't appear so at first glance, this move was actually part of an economy drive.

"In 1959," explains Clare MacKichan, "we went to a shared body shell with Pontiac, Olds and Buick. This was an effort to save money in the corporation. The idea was to make the outer surfaces different so that nobody would know they were shared, but the things underneath that cost the major amount of money *would* be shared." Asked what Chevy might have gone with had this decision not been made, MacKichan says, "I suppose there were facelifts made, but I don't know where they are or what they were. I think the idea of going to a new body shell came very early, so we did not do much on a facelift."

Notes Carl Renner, "Designs have to wear well, be ever-lasting. I will give you a good example on an early 1959 Chevrolet front end design proposal which was a center theme with a double headlight, one over the other. It was a motif like the Edsel's central grille, or the Tucker's third headlight. It was mocked up and ready to go; fortunately they did not come out with it." Considering the success of the Edsel and the Tucker, it probably is well they didn't!

But there are many who believe the 1959 Chevrolet wasn't a very good thing anyway. Unquestionably it marked the advent of larger, heavier Chevys that were the Division's "standard cars" right on through 1976--only to be eliminated in 1977 by the advent of expensive oil and government mandates for fuel economy. The Impala for 1959 was now a separate series, as it has been ever since. The Bel Air was downgraded to the middle model, the Biscayne dropped down to replace Delray. Wheelbases were stretched again, and the cars were larger in every dimension. The changes wrought between 1957 and 1959 are quite startling:

	1957	1958	1959
Wheelbase (inches)	115	117.5	119
length (inches)	200	209.1	210.9
width (inches)	73.9	77.7	79.9
height, hardtop (inches)	58.5	57.4	54.0
weight, top sedan (lbs.)	3336	3475	3630

Aside from styling, the 1959s offered still more potent engines, up to 315 horsepower; air suspension was still available though not talked about, and would be dropped for 1960. But the styling, with big, curved fins (falsely rumored to lift the rear end off the ground at high speed) and a massively wide deck (McCahill: "Enough room to land a Piper Cub") were detriments to really good sales. Ford finally outsold Chevrolet by 100,000 cars.

The fins decreased in size for 1960, and were gone completely by 1961, so the 1959 ranks as the most radical Chevrolet of the tail fin era. In terms of sales appeal at least, it was one of the least successful. The one and one-half million that did sell were an improvement on dismal 1958, but decidedly less than every year since 1954. In 1960, though, Chevy was number one again, and had increased sales to a record 1,873,598; in 1962 the figure topped two million for the first time, and remained at or above that figure through 1966.

But the story written in those wide, curvaceous fins, excess poundage and growing dimensions was clear, and the

The production 1959 Impala sport sedan, as it stood on April 18, 1958, wearing its accessory rocker panel molding, and whitewalls.

By 1961, the Chevrolet Nomad and other models had shed 1959-60's tail fins. (Car shown used 1959 wheel covers, non-stock bumper).

story was that by 1959 the era of the Hot One had irrevocably ended. Chevrolet would continue to build hot cars --its 409 cubic inch, 409 hp model of 1962 is a typical example--but excepting Corvette they were generally large, heavy, "full-size" automobiles.

Meanwhile a new era of diversification was dawning to meet the needs of the times, and those buyers for whom 115 inches was sufficient wheelbase. The compact, rear engined Corvair was Chevrolet's introduction for 1960, and before long a sporty version of same called Monza was seen to open a brand new market which Chevy was fast to exploit--the small, sporty, four-seat "pony cars." The Cor-

vair did quite well in this field until eclipsed in the late Sixties by Ford's Mustang and Chevy's own Camaro.

There were many other Chevrolet innovations in the Sixties and early Seventies that invoked this whole new approach to Divisional affairs: Chevy II, compact response to the conventional Ford Falcon in 1962 (it has since sold, as the Nova after 1969, over 3.5 million copies); Chevelle, a parallel development of the earlier, intermediate Fairlane, introduced with success in 1964; the aforementioned Camaro, in 1967; the notably unreliable and unsuccessful Vega, a subcompact 1970 introduction recently phased out of production; the splendidly styled "new" Monza of

1975; the small and economical Chevette, meeting the needs of the mid-Seventies in 1975 as a 1976 model. Today Chevrolet Division alone echoes Alfred P. Sloan's ancient dictum for the whole of General Motors. "A car for every price and pocketbook" is offered by one of the most formidable automotive conglomerates in the world. And Chevy is only part of an even bigger conglomerate, GM itself, which is now striking out for 60 percent of the American market.

For the decade and a half between 1960 and 1975, the name Impala was as ubiquitous as hamburgers and ice cream. Today, on new, sensibly sized Chevrolets, it remains with us yet, though one step down from the most recent Caprice; at 20 years of age in 1978, it's one of the longest running model designations. If it stood in the minds of enthusiastic drivers as the symbol of how unnecessarily large American cars grew to be, it is also--now --the symbol of how ready Chevrolet Division is to meet the times. This characteristic, intrinsic to Chevy throughout most of its history, is probably the single largest reason why the Division is where it is today, and unlikely to be challenged in the foreseeable future.

Corporately, of course, the history of Chevrolet is not one of any particular series of cars. It is a history of al-most steady success, of unparalleled growth and prosperity for hundreds of thousands who've been part of it, from the assemblers on the production line to the engineer at the drafting board and the stylist in the clay model room. It has long since earned the right to wear its famous license plate trademark, USA-1--because it *is* USA-1. Chevrolet has always offered what the average American was looking for--be it basic transportation, sports car panache, compact economy, a comfortable intermediate, an exciting innovator like the Corvair Monza. As top dog, Chevy will always be criticized, analyzed, second-guessed and pilloried by those who think they know better. And Chevy will just as inevitably go on making money, and supporting a sizeable sector of the American economy. Which is all to the good.

But the 1955-57 Chevy was unquestionably a high point in a history of many successes. The Hot One was a car as right for the times as Corvair was for 1960, as Chevette was for 1975. Beyond that, it combined exciting performance with really excellent styling, good workmanship and good looks. And you can't ask for much more than that in any car. One commentator at least saw all this even as the '55 was introduced. "This," he said, "may be judged by historians as one of the great Chevys of all time."

It was.

Appendix

APPENDIX I   U.S. CALENDAR YEAR PRODUCTION 1945-1960

1945

1. Ford	34,439
2. Chevrolet	12,776
3. Nash	6,148
4. Pontiac	5,606
5. Hudson	4,735
6. Oldsmobile	3,498
7. Mercury	2,848
8. Packard	2,722
9. Buick	2,482
10. Cadillac	1,142
11. DeSoto	947
12. Plymouth	770
13. Studebaker	651
14. Lincoln	500
15. Dodge	420
16. Chrysler	322

1946

1. Chevrolet	397,104
2. Ford	372,917
3. Plymouth	242,534
4. Dodge	156,128
5. Buick	156,080
6. Pontiac	131,538
7. Oldsmobile	114,674
8. Nash	98,769
9. Hudson	90,766
10. Studebaker	77,567
11. Chrysler	76,753
12. Mercury	70,955
13. DeSoto	62,860
14. Packard	42,102
15. Cadillac	28,144
16. Lincoln	13,487

1947

1. Chevrolet	695,986
2. Ford	601,665
3. Plymouth	350,327
4. Buick	267,830
5. Dodge	232,216
6. Pontiac	223,015
7. Oldsmobile	191,454
8. Kaiser-Frazer	144,490
9. Mercury	124,612
10. Studebaker	123,642
11. Nash	113,315
12. Chrysler	109,195
13. Hudson	100,393
14. DeSoto	81,752
15. Cadillac	59,436
16. Packard	55,477
17. Willys	33,214
18. Lincoln	29,097
19. Crosley	16,162

1948

1. Chevrolet	775,982
2. Ford	549,077
3. Plymouth	378,048
4. Buick	275,504
5. Pontiac	253,469
6. Dodge	232,390
7. Oldsmobile	194,755
8. Kaiser-Frazer	181,316
9. Studebaker	164,753
10. Mercury	154,702
11. Hudson	143,697
12. Chrysler	119,137
13. Nash	118,621
14. Packard	98,898
15. DeSoto	92,920
16. Cadillac	66,209
17. Lincoln	43,938
18. Willys	32,635
19. Crosley	24,871

1949

1.	Chevrolet	1,109,958
2.	Ford	841,170
3.	Plymouth	574,734
4.	Buick	398,482
5.	Pontiac	333,954
6.	Dodge	298,399
7.	Oldsmobile	282,887
8.	Studebaker	228,402
9.	Mercury	203,339
10.	Nash	142,592
11.	Hudson	142,462
12.	Chrysler	141,122
13.	DeSoto	108,440
14.	Packard	104,593
15.	Cadillac	81,545
16.	Kaiser-Frazer	57,995
17.	Lincoln	33,132
18.	Willys	32,928
19.	Crosley	8,549

1950

1.	Chevrolet	1,520,577
2.	Ford	1,187,122
3.	Plymouth	573,116
4.	Buick	552,827
5.	Pontiac	467,655
6.	Oldsmobile	396,757
7.	Mercury	334,081
8.	Dodge	332,782
9.	Studebaker	268,099
10.	Nash	189,543
11.	Chrysler	167,316
12.	Kaiser-Frazer	146,911
13.	Hudson	143,006
14.	DeSoto	127,557
15.	Cadillac	110,535
16.	Packard	72,138
17.	Willys	38,052
18.	Lincoln	35,485
19.	Crosley	7,043

1951

1.	Chevrolet	1,118,096
2.	Ford	900,770
3.	Plymouth	621,013
4.	Buick	404,657
5.	Pontiac	343,795
6.	Dodge	325,694
7.	Oldsmobile	285,634
8.	Mercury	238,854
9.	Studebaker	222,000
10.	Chrysler	162,916
11.	Nash-Rambler	161,140
12.	DeSoto	121,794
13.	Cadillac	103,266
14.	Kaiser-Fraser	99,343
15.	Hudson	93,327
16.	Packard	76,075
17.	Willys	28,226
18.	Lincoln	25,386
19.	Crosley	4,839

1952

1.	Chevrolet	877,947
2.	Ford	777,531
3.	Plymouth	474,836
4.	Buick	321,048
5.	Pontiac	277,156
6.	Dodge	259,519
7.	Oldsmobile	228,452
8.	Mercury	195,261
9.	Studebaker	161,520
10.	Nash-Rambler	152,141
11.	Chrysler	120,678
12.	DeSoto	97,558
13.	Cadillac	96,850
14.	Hudson	76,348
15.	Kaiser	71,306
16.	Packard	62,988
17.	Willys	48,845
18.	Lincoln	31,992
19.	Crosley	1,522

1953

1.	Chevrolet	1,477,287
2.	Ford	1,184,187
3.	Plymouth	662,515
4.	Buick	485,353
5.	Pontiac	414,011
6.	Mercury	320,369
7.	Oldsmobile	319,414
8.	Dodge	293,714
9.	Studebaker	186,484
10.	Chrysler	160,410
11.	Nash-Rambler	135,394
12.	DeSoto	129,963
13.	Cadillac	103,538
14.	Packard	81,341
15.	Hudson	76,348
16.	Lincoln	41,962
17.	Willys	40,563
18.	Kaiser	21,686

1954

1.	Chevrolet	1,414,352
2.	Ford	1,394,762
3.	Buick	531,463
4.	Oldsmobile	433,810
5.	Plymouth	399,900
6.	Pontiac	370,887
7.	Mercury	256,730
8.	Dodge	151,766
9.	Cadillac	123,746
10.	Chrysler	101,745
11.	Studebaker	82,252
12.	DeSoto	69,844
13.	Nash-Rambler	62,911
14.	Lincoln	35,733
15.	Hudson	32,287
16.	Packard	27,593
17.	Kaiser-Willys	16,759

187

1955

1.	Chevrolet	1,830,038
2.	Ford	1,764,524
3.	Buick	781,296
4.	Plymouth	742,991
5.	Oldsmobile	643,460
6.	Pontiac	581,860
7.	Mercury	434,911
8.	Dodge	313,038
9.	Chrysler	176,039
10.	Am. Motors	161,790
11.	Cadillac	153,334
12.	DeSoto	129,767
13.	Studebaker	112,392
14.	Packard	69,667
15.	Lincoln-Contl.	41,226
16.	Imperial	13,727

1956

1.	Chevrolet	1,621,005
2.	Ford	1,373,542
3.	Buick	535,364
4.	Plymouth	452,958
5.	Oldsmobile	432,904
6.	Pontiac	332,268
7.	Mercury	246,629
8.	Dodge	205,727
9.	Cadillac	140,873
10.	Am. Motors	104,190
11.	DeSoto	104,090
12.	Chrysler	95,356
13.	Studebaker	82,402
14.	Lincoln-Contl.	48,995
15.	Packard	13,432
16.	Imperial	12,130

1957

1.	Chevrolet	1,522,536
2.	Ford	1,522,406
3.	Plymouth	655,526
4.	Buick	407,271
5.	Oldsmobile	390,091
6.	Pontiac	343,298
7.	Dodge	292,386
8.	Mercury	274,820
9.	Cadillac	153,236
10.	Chrysler	118,733
11.	DeSoto	117,747
12.	Am. Motors	114,084
13.	Stude-Packard	72,889
14.	Edsel	54,607
15.	Imperial	37,946
16.	Lincoln-Contl.	37,870

1958

1.	Chevrolet	1,255,935
2.	Ford	1,038,560
3.	Plymouth	367,296
4.	Oldsmobile	310,795
5.	Buick	257,124
6.	Pontiac	219,823
7.	Rambler	217,332
8.	Mercury	128,428
9.	Cadillac	125,501
10.	Dodge	114,206
11.	Stude-Packard	56,869
12.	Chrysler	49,513
13.	DeSoto	36,556
14.	Edsel	26,563
15.	Lincoln	25,871
16.	Imperial	13,673

1959

1.	Ford	1,528,592
2.	Chevrolet	1,428,962
3.	Plymouth	413,204
4.	Rambler	401,446
5.	Pontiac	388,856
6.	Oldsmobile	366,305
7.	Buick	232,579
8.	Dodge	192,798
9.	Mercury	156,765
10.	Studebaker	153,823
11.	Cadillac	138,527
12.	Chrysler	69,411
13.	DeSoto	41,423
14.	Lincoln	30,375
15.	Edsel	29,667
16.	Imperial	20,963

1960

1.	Chevrolet	1,873,598
2.	Ford	1,511,504
3.	Rambler	485,745
4.	Plymouth	483,969
5.	Pontiac	450,206
6.	Dodge	411,666
7.	Oldsmobile	402,612
8.	Mercury	359,818
9.	Buick	307,804
10.	Cadillac	158,941
11.	Studebaker	105,902
12.	Chrysler	87,420
13.	Lincoln	20,683
14.	DeSoto	19,411
15.	Imperial	16,829
16.	Checker	6,980

APPENDIX II   INDUSTRY PERCENTAGES FOR BIG THREE, 1949-1957 (WARD'S)

	1949	*1950*	*1951*	*1952*	*1953*	*1954*	*1955*	*1956*	*1957*
Chevrolet	21.64	22.78	20.94	20.24	24.08	25.67	23.04	27.94	24.90
Ford	16.40	17.79	16.87	17.93	19.30	25.31	22.22	23.68	24.89
Plymouth	11.21	8.59	11.63	10.95	10.80	7.26	9.36	7.81	10.73

APPENDIX III   1955 MODELS

1955 CHEVROLET

Model Number	Body Style (passengers)	Production	Price*	Weight (lbs)*
One-Fifty				
1502	sedan, 2dr (6)	66,416	$1784	3080
1503	sedan, 4dr (6)	29,898	1827	3135
1512	sedan, 2dr utility (3)	11,196	1692	3055
1529	Handyman wagon, 2dr (6)	17,936	2129	3260
	Total	125,446		
Two-Ten				
2102	sedan, 2dr (6)	249,105	1874	3115
2103	sedan, 4dr (6)	317,724	1918	3150
2124	Delray club coupe (6)	115,584	1934	3115
2154	sport coupe (6)	11,675	2058	3140
2129	Handyman wagon, 2dr (6)	28,918	2178	3300
2109	**Townsman** wagon, 4 dr (6)	82,303	2226	3340
	Total	805,309		
Bel Air				
2402	sedan, 2dr (6)	168,313	1987	3125
2403	sedan, 4dr (6)	345,372	2031	3170
2454	sport coupe (6)	185,562	2166	3165
2434	convertible (5)	41,292	2305	3285
2429	Nomad wagon, 2 dr (6)	8,530	2571	3335
2409	Beauville wagon, 4dr (6)	24,313	2361	3355
	Total	773,382		

*All prices, weights and model numbers for cars equipped with standard V-8 manual transmission. Six cylinder models about $100 lower.

1955 ENGINE DATA AND POWER TEAMS

Engine	Models	Cu. In. Displ.	Comp. Ratio	Bore	Stroke	Gross H.P.	Net H.P.	Carburetor	Transmission
Blue Flame 123 — 6 cyl.	PASS.	235	7.5	3-9/16"	3-15/16"	123 @ 3800 RPM	109 @ 3600 RPM	Single Barrel	3-Speed Overdrive
Blue Flame 136 — 6 cyl.	PASS.	235	7.5	3-9/16"	3-15/16"	136 @ 4200 RPM	121 @ 3800 RPM	Single Barrel	Powerglide
Turbo-Fire 8 cyl.	PASS.	265	8.0	3-3/4"	3"	162 @ 4400 RPM	137 @ 4000 RPM	2-Barrel	3-Speed Overdrive Powerglide
Turbo-Fire 8 cyl.	PASS.	265	8.0	3-3/4"	3"	180 @ 4600 RPM	160 @ 4200 RPM	4-Barrel	3-Speed Overdrive Powerglide

1955 DIMENSIONS

Dimensions (inches): Wheelbase 115; overall length 195.6 (station wagons 197.1); overall height 60.5 (hardtop/convertible 59.1, station wagons 60.8, Nomad 60.7); overall width 74; front track 58; rear track 58.8; ground clearance 6.5.

1955 ACCESSORIES

Fender antenna, self-de-icing wiper blade, wiring junction block, locking gas cap, Continental wheel carrier, electric clock, compass, nylon/plastic/fiber seat covers, accelerator pedal cover, wheel covers, wire wheel covers, tissue dispenser, exhaust extension, filter and element, license plate frame, glareshades, grille guard, fender guard, door edge guard, gasoline filler guard, heater & defroster, tool kit, back-up lamps, courtesy lamps, cigarette lighter, floor mats, outside rearview mirrors, inside non-glare rearview mirrors, vanity visor, body sill, radio (manual, push-button, signal seeking), automatic top raiser, arm rests, wheel trim rings, safetylight with mirror, spotlamp, electric shaver, parking brake signal, door handle shields, front fender shields, rear seat speaker, ventshades, outside visors, inside visors, traffic light viewer, windshield washer (vacuum or foot), air conditioning.

1955 TRIM COMBINATION CHART

Comb. No.	Materials	Models
500	Light Gray Pattern Cloth	1200 (exc. Sta. Wag. Sdl.)
547	Light Gray—Black Imitation Leather	1211
506	Light Blue—Beige Imitation Leather	1011A
507	Light Green—Beige Imitation Leather	1011A
508	Black—Ivory Imitation Leather	1011A
503	Light Blue Pattern—Dark Blue Plain Cloth	1011-19-37
504	Light Green Pattern—Dark Green Plain Cloth	1011-19-37
505	Light Tan Pattern—Dark Brown Plain Cloth	1011-19-37
509	Dark Blue Pattern Cloth—Light Blue Imitation Leather	1011D-19D
510	Dark Green Pattern Cloth—Light Green Imitation Leather	1011D-19D
511	Dark Brown Pattern Cloth—Beige Imitation Leather	1011D-19D
513	Turquoise Pattern Cloth—Ivory Imitation Leather	1011D-19D
531	Dark Gray Pattern Cloth—Coral Imitation Leather	1011D-19D
549	Dark Gray Pattern Cloth—Ivory Imitation Leather	1011D-19D
525	Red—Beige Imitation Leather	Conv.
526	Dark Green—Light Green Imitation Leather	Conv.
527	Dark Blue—Light Blue Imitation Leather	Conv.
528	Brown—Beige Imitation Leather	Conv.
533	Dark Gray—Coral Imitation Leather	Conv.
537	Turquoise—Ivory Imitation Leather	Conv.
551	Dark Gray—Ivory Imitation Leather	Conv.
519	Beige Pattern Cloth—Light Blue Imitation Leather	1037D
520	Beige Pattern Cloth—Light Green Imitation Leather	1037D
521	Beige Pattern Cloth—Red Imitation Leather	1037D
522	Beige Pattern Cloth—Turquoise Imitation Leather	1037D
532	Gray Pattern Cloth—Coral Imitation Leather	1037D
550	Gray Pattern Cloth—Ivory Imitation Leather	1037D
514	Light Blue-Beige Imitation Leather	1062F-63F
515	Dark Green—Light Green Imitation Leather	1062F-63F
516	Brown—Beige Imitation Leather	1062F-63F
517	Beige Pattern Cloth—Beige Imitation Leather	1062DF
518	Beige Pattern Cloth—Light Blue Imitation Leather	1062DF
502	Straw—Brown Imitation Leather	1263F
524	Dark Green—Light Green Imitation Leather	1263F
501	Straw—Brown Imitation Leather	Sdl.
541	Beige and Green Leather	Nomad
542	Beige and Blue Leather	Nomad
543	Beige and Brown Leather	Nomad
544	Beige and Red Leather	Nomad
545	Ivory and Turquoise Leather	Nomad
546	Gray and Coral Leather	Nomad
552	Gray and Ivory Leather	Nomad

1955 PAINT COMBINATION CHART

Comb. No.	Model Usage	Body Color	Duco No.	Wheel Color Color	Dulux No.	Wheel Striping Color	Duco No.
585	1011-11A-19-1211-11B-19-71	Onyx Black	253 2247	Black	505	Argent Silver	2894202
585	1011D-19D-37D-67D	Onyx Black	253 2247	Black	505	None	
586	1011-11A-19-1200 Series	Sea Mist Green	253 57950	Sea Mist Green	670	Onyx Black	2532247
586	1011D-19D-67D	Sea Mist Green	253 57950	Sea Mist Green	670	None	
587	1011-11A-19-62F-63F-1200 Series	Neptune Green	281 57951	Neptune Green	671	Argent Silver	2894202
587	1011D-19D-37D-62DF	Neptune Green	281 57951	Neptune Green	671	None	
588	1011-11A-19-1211-11B-19-71	Skyline Blue	253 58001	Skyline Blue	680	Onyx Black	2532247
588	1011D-19D-67D	Skyline Blue	253 58001	Skyline Blue	680	None	
589	1011-11A-19-62F-63F-1211-11B-19-71	Glacier Blue	281 57921	Glacier Blue	676	Argent Silver	2894202
589	1011D-19D-37D-62DF	Glacier Blue	281 57921	Glacier Blue	676	None	
590	1011-19-1211-11B-19-71	Copper Maroon	281 58099	Copper Maroon	678	Argent Silver	2894202
590	1011D-19D	Copper Maroon	281 58099	Copper Maroon	678	None	
591	1011-19-62F-63F-1211-11B-19	Shoreline Beige	253 57602	Shoreline Beige	647	Onyx Black	2532247
591	Bel Air	Shoreline Beige	253 57602	Shoreline Beige	647	None	
592	1011-19-62F-1211-11B-19-63F	Autumn Bronze	281 58009	Autumn Bronze	672	Argent Silver	2894202
592	1067D	Autumn Bronze	281 58009	Autumn Bronze	672	None	
593	1011-11A-19-1211-11B-19-71	India Ivory	253 58458	India Ivory	689	Onyx Black	2532247
593	1011D-19D	India Ivory	253 58458	India Ivory	689	None	
594	1011-19-1211-11B-19-71	Shadow Gray	286 57631	Shadow Gray	654	Argent Silver	2894202
594	1011D-19D	Shadow Gray	286 57631	Shadow Gray	654	None	
596	Conv.	Gypsy Red	253 57953	Gypsy Red	673	None	
598	1062DF-67D	Regal Turquoise	281 57955	Regal Turquoise	675	None	
626	Conv.	Coral	253 57990	Coral	679	None	
630	Spt. Cpe.	Harvest Gold	253 58456	Harvest Gold	698	None	
683	1011-11A-19-1211-11B-19-71	Cashmere Blue	253 58455	Cashmere Blue	699	Onyx Black	2532247
	1011D-19D	Cashmere Blue	253 58455	Cashmere Blue	699	None	

1955 TWO TONE COLOR COMBINATIONS

Comb. No.	Model Usage	Upper Body		Lower Body		Wheel Color		Wheel Striping	
		Color	Duco No.	Color	Duco No.	Color	Dulux No.	Color	Duco N
599	1011-19-62F-63F 1211-19-63F	Sea Mist Green	25357950	Neptune Green	28157951	Neptune Green	671	Argent Silver	28942(
599	1011D-19D	Sea Mist Green	25357950	Neptune Green	28157951	Neptune Green	671	None	
600	1011-19-1211-19	Skyline Blue	25358001	Glacier Blue	28157921	Glacier Blue	676	Argent Silver	28942(
600	1011D-19D	Skyline Blue	25358001	Glacier Blue	28157921	Glacier Blue	676	None	
601	Spt. Cpe.	Neptune Green	28157951	Shoreline Beige	25357602	Shoreline Beige	647	None	
602	1011-11A-19-1211-1219	India Ivory	25358458	Skyline Blue	25358001	Skyline Blue	680	Onyx Black	253224
602	1011D-19D-37D	India Ivory	25358458	Skyline Blue	25358001	Skyline Blue	680	None	
603	1062F-63F	Autumn Bronze	28158009	Shoreline Beige	25357602	Shoreline Beige	647	Onyx Black	253224
604	1062DF-67D	Neptune Green	28157951	Sea Mist Green	25357950	Sea Mist Green	670	None	
605	1011-11A-19	India Ivory	25358458	Sea Mist Green	25357950	Sea Mist Green	670	Onyx Black	253224
606	1011-19-1263F	Shoreline Beige	25357602	Autumn Bronze	28158009	Autumn Bronze	672	Argent Silver	28942(
606	1011D-19D-37D-62DF	Shoreline Beige	25357602	Autumn Bronze	28158009	Autumn Bronze	672	None	
607	1011-11A-19	Glacier Blue	28157921	Shoreline Beige	25357602	Shoreline Beige	647	Onyx Black	253224
608	1011A	India Ivory	25358458	Onyx Black	2532247	Black	505	Argent Silver	28942(
608	1011D-19D-37D-67D	India Ivory	25358458	Onyx Black	2532247	Black	505	None	
610	1062F-63F	Glacier Blue	28157921	Skyline Blue	25358001	Skyline Blue	680	Onyx Black	253224
610	Conv.	Glacier Blue	28157921	Skyline Blue	25358001	Skyline Blue	680	None	
612	1011D-19D-37D-67D	India Ivory	25358458	Regal Turquoise	28157955	Regal Turquoise	675	None	
613	1011-19-1211-11B-19	Shoreline Beige	25357602	Neptune Green	28157951	Neptune Green	671	Argent Silver	28942(
613	1011D-19D-37D	Shoreline Beige	25357602	Neptune Green	28157951	Neptune Green	671	None	
614	1011-11A-19-62F-63F-1211-19	Shoreline Beige	25357602	Glacier Blue	28157921	Glacier Blue	676	Argent Silver	28942(
614	1011D-19D-37D-62DF	Shoreline Beige	25357602	Glacier Blue	28157921	Glacier Blue	676	None	
615	1037D-62DF-67D	Shoreline Beige	25357602	Gypsy Red	25357953	Gypsy Red	673	None	
617	1011A	India Ivory	25358458	Gypsy Red	25357953	Gypsy Red	673	Argent Silver	28942(
624	1011-19-1211-11B-19	India Ivory	25358458	Shadow Gray	28657631	Shadow Gray	654	Argent Silver	28942(
624	1011D-19D	India Ivory	25358458	Shadow Gray	28657631	Shadow Gray	654	None	
627	1011D-19D-37D-64DF-67D	Shadow Gray	28657631	Coral	25357990	Coral	679	None	
628	1011A	Onyx Black	2532247	India Ivory	25358458	India Ivory	689	Onyx Black	253224
628	1011D-19D-37D	Onyx Black	2532247	India Ivory	25358458	India Ivory	689	None	
629	Conv.	India Ivory	25358458	Coral	25357990	Coral	679	None	
631	1011A	India Ivory	25358458	Harvest Gold	25358456	Harvest Gold	698	Onyx Black	253224
631	1011D-19D-37D-67D	India Ivory	25358458	Harvest Gold	25358456	Harvest Gold	698	None	
682	1011-11A-19-62F-63F-1211-19	India Ivory	25358458	Cashmere Blue	25358455	Cashmere Blue	699	Onyx Black	253224
682	1011D-19D-37D-62DF-64DF-67D	India Ivory	25358458	Cashmere Blue	25358455	Cashmere Blue	699	None	
684	1011-19-62F-63F-1263F	India Ivory	25358458	Navajo Tan	28158457	Navajo Tan	700	Onyx Black	25322
684	1011D-19D-37D-62DF-64DF-67D	India Ivory	25358458	Navajo Tan	28158457	Navajo Tan	700	None	
685	1011D-19D-37D-64DF-67D	India Ivory	25358458	Dusk-Rose	28658459	Dusk-Rose	690	None	

APPENDIX IV 1956 MODELS

1956 CHEVROLET

Model Number	Body Style (passengers)	Production	Price [*]	Weight (lbs) [*]
One-Fifty				
1502	sedan, 2 dr (6)	82,384	$1925	3144
1503	sedan, 4dr (6)	51,544	1968	3186
1512	sedan, 2dr utility (3)	9,879	1833	3107
1529	Handyman wagon, 2 dr (6)	13,487	2270	3289
	Total	157,294		
Two-Ten				
2102	sedan, 2dr (6)	205,545	2011	3157
2103	sedan, 4dr (6)	283,125	2054	3192
2124	Delray club coupe (6)	56,382	2070	3162
2154	sport coupe (6)	18,616	2162	3184
2113	sport sedan (6)	20,021	2216	3242
2129	Handyman wagon, 2dr (6)	22,038	2314	3324
2109	Townsman wagon, 4dr (6)	113,656	2362	3361
2119	Beauville wagon, 4 dr (9)	17,988	2447	3480
	Total	737,371		
Bel Air				
2402	sedan, 2dr (6)	104,849	2124	3177
2403	sedan, 4dr (6)	269,798	2167	3211
2454	sport coupe (6)	128,382	2275	3212
2413	sport sedan (6)	103,602	2329	3260
2434	convertible (5)	41,268	2443	3320
2429	Nomad wagon, 2dr (6)	8,103	2707	3342
2419	Beauville wagon, 4dr (9)	13,279	2581	3496
	Total	669,281		

[*] All prices, weights and model numbers for cars equipped with standard V-8 manual transmission. Six cylinder models about $100 lower.

1956 ENGINE DATA AND POWER TEAMS

Engine	Models	Cu. In. Displ.	Comp. Ratio	Bore	Stroke	Gross H.P.	Net H.P.	Carburetor	Transmission
Blue Flame 140 — 6 cyl.	PASS.	235	8.0	3-9/16"	3-15/16"	140 @ 4200 RPM	125 @ 4000 RPM	Single Barrel	3-Speed Overdrive Powerglide
Turbo-Fire 162 — 8 cyl	PASS.	265	8.0	3-3/4"	3"	162 @ 4400 RPM	137 @ 4000 RPM	2-Barrel	3-Speed Overdrive
Turbo-Fire 170 — 8 cyl.	PASS.	265	8.0	3-3/4"	3"	170 @ 4400 RPM	141 @ 4000 RPM	2-Barrel	Powerglide
Turbo-Fire 205 — 8 cyl	PASS.	265	8.0	3-3/4"	3"	205 @ 4600 RPM	170 @ 4200 RPM	4-Barrel	3-Speed Overdrive Powerglide
Turbo-Fire 225 — 8 cyl.	PASS.	265	9.25	3-3/4"	3"	225 @ 5200 RPM	196 @ 4800 RPM	Dual 4-Barrel	3-Speed Overdrive Powerglide

1956 DIMENSIONS

Dimensions (inches): Wheelbase 115; overall length 197.5 (station wagons 200.8); overall height 60.5 (hardtop/convertible 59.1, station wagons 60.8, Nomad 60.7); overall width 74 (hardtops and convertible 72.9, station wagons 74); front track 58; rear track 58.8; ground clearance 6.5.

1956 ACCESSORIES

Air conditioning, fender antenna, Autronic Eye headlamp control, seatbelts, self-de-icing wiper blade, wiring junction block, power brakes, locking gas cap, Continental wheel carrier, electric clock, compass, nylon/plastic/fiber seat covers, accelerator pedal cover, wheel covers, wire wheel covers, tissue dispenser, exhaust extension, license plate frame, glareshades, fender guards, door edge guards, heater & defroster, vibrator horn, tool kit, Kool Kooshions, back-up lamps, courtesy lamps, cigarette lighter, floor mats, outside rearview mirror, non-glare rearview mirror, visor vanity mirror, body sill moulding, front fender top moulding, radio (manual, pushbutton, signal seeking), automatic top raiser, armrests, safetylight & mirror, radiator insect screen, spotlamp, electric shaver, door handle shield, front fender shield, rear seat speaker, ventshades, outside visor, inside visors, traffic light viewer, windshield washer (coordinated or foot-operated).

1956 TRIM COMBINATION CHART

Comb. No.	Material	Models
560	Gold Dotted Black Cloth Gold Striped Imitation Leather	1200 (exc. Sta. Wag. Sdl.)
567	Black Ivory Imitation Leather	1011A
568	Green Ivory Imitation Leather	1011A
569	Turquoise Ivory Imitation Leather	1011A
564	Charcoal Pattern Cloth-Starfrost	1011-19-37-39
565	Green Pattern Cloth—Starfrost	1011-19-37-39
566	Blue Pattern Cloth-Starfrost	1011-19-37-39
573	Charcoal Pattern Cloth Ivory Imitation Leather	1011D-19D
574	Green Pattern Cloth Green Imitation Leather	1011D-19D
575	Blue Pattern Cloth Blue Imitation Leather	1011D-19D
577	Turquoise Pattern Cloth Turquoise Imitation Leather	1011D-19D
578	Charcoal Pattern Cloth Yellow Imitation Leather	1011D-19D
617	Copper Pattern Cloth Tan Imitation Leather	1011D-19D
626	Charcoal Pattern Cloth Cream Imitation Leather	1011D, 1019D
602	Charcoal—Ivory Imitation Leather	Conv.
603	Turquoise—Ivory Imitation Leather	Conv.
604	Charcoal—Yellow Imitation Leather	Conv.
605	Red—Ivory Imitation Leather	Conv.
606	Medium Green—Light Green Imitation Leather	Conv.
607	Medium Blue—Light Blue Imitation Leather	Conv.
621	Copper—Tan Imitation Leather	Conv.
631	Charcoal Imitation Leather Cream Imitation Leather	Conv.
579	Charcoal Pattern Cloth Ivory Imitation Leather	1037D-39D
610	Charcoal Pattern Cloth Ivory Imitation Leather	1062DF
629	Red Taupe Pattern Cloth Red Imitation Leather	1062DF (Replaces 586)
630	Charcoal Yellow Pattern Cloth Cream Imitation Leather	1062DF
611	Charcoal Pattern Cloth	
	Ivory Imitation Leather	1064
632	Charcoal Yellow Pattern Cloth Cream Imitation Leather	1064
633	Red Taupe Pattern Cloth Red Imitation Leather	1064
580	Medium Green Pattern Cloth Light Green Imitation Leather	1037-39D
590	Medium Green Pattern Cloth Light Green Imitation Leather	1064
581	Medium Blue Pattern Cloth Light Blue Imitation Leather	1037D-39D
591	Light Blue Pattern Cloth Light Blue Imitation Leather	1064
627	Charcoal Yellow Pattern Cloth Cream Imitation Leather	1037D, 1039D
628	Red Taupe Pattern Cloth Red Imitation Leather	1039D (Replaces 583)
593	Red Pattern Cloth Red Imitation Leather	1064
584	Medium Turquoise Pattern Cloth—Light Turquoise Imitation Leather	1037D
587	Medium Turquoise Pattern Cloth—Light Turquoise Imitation Leather	1062DF
594	Medium Turquoise Pattern Cloth—Light Turquoise Imitation Leather	1064
585	Charcoal Pattern Cloth Yellow Imitation Leather	1037D-39D
588	Charcoal Pattern Cloth Yellow Imitation Leather	1062DF
595	Charcoal Pattern Cloth Yellow Imitation Leather	1064
618	Tan Pattern Cloth Copper Imitation Leather	1037D-39D
619	Tan Pattern Cloth Copper Imitation Leather	1062DF
620	Tan Pattern Cloth Copper Imitation Leather	1064
570	Medium Green Imitation Leather—Starfrost	1062F-62FC-63F
572	Medium Turquoise Imitation Leather—Starfrost	1062F-62FC-63F
609	Charcoal Imitation Leather—Starfrost	1062F-62FC-63F
562	Medium Green—Gold Striped Imitation Leather	1263F
616	Charcoal Gray—Gold Striped Imitation Leather	1263F
615	Charcoal Gray—Gold Striped Imitation Leather	1271

1956 PAINT COMBINATION CHART

Comb. No.	Model Usage	Body		Wheel Color		Wheel Striping	
		Color	*Duco No.*	*Color*	*Dulux No.*	*Color*	*Duco No.*
687	All Models	Onyx Black	253 2247	Black	505	Argent Silver	2894202
688	150, 210 Series	Pinecrest Green	253 58897	Pinecrest Green	716	Onyx Black	2532247
688	1011D-19D-37D-39D-62DF-67D	Pinecrest Green	253 58897	Pinecrest Green	716	None	
690	150, 210 Series	Sherwood Green	286 59525	Sherwood Green	717	Argent Silver	2894202
690	1011D-19D-37D-39D-67D	Sherwood Green	286 59525	Sherwood Green	717	None	
691	150, 210 Series	Nassau Blue	253 58752	Nassau Blue	718	Onyx Black	2532247
691	1011D-19D-37D-39D-62DF-67D	Nassau Blue	253 58752	Nassau Blue	718	None	
692	1011-19-37-39-1271	Harbor Blue	281 58812	Harbor Blue	719	Argent Silver	2894202
692	1011D-19D-37D-39D-67D	Harbor Blue	281 58812	Harbor Blue	719	None	
693	1011-11A-19-37-39	Dusk Plum	281 59238	Dusk Plum	728	Argent Silver	2894202
693	1011D-19D-37D-39D-62DF-67D	Dusk Plum	281 59238	Dusk Plum	728	None	
694	150, 210 Series	India Ivory	253 58458	India Ivory	689	Onyx Black	2532247
694	1011D-19D-37D-39D-62DF-67D	India Ivory	253 58458	India Ivory	689	None	
695	150 (exc. 1271), 210 Series	Crocus Yellow	253 58763	Crocus Yellow	725	Onyx Black	2532247
695	1011D-19D-37D-39D-62DF-67D	Crocus Yellow	253 58763	Crocus Yellow	725	None	
697	150 (exc. 1263F), 210 Series	Matador Red	253 59446	Matador Red	738	Onyx Black	2532247
697	1011D-19D-37D-39D-62DF-67D	Matador Red	253 59446	Matador Red	738	None	
698	210 Series—1211-11B-19	Twilight Turquoise	253 58920	Twilight Turquoise	723	Argent Silver	2894202
698	1011D-19D-37D-39D-62DF-67D	Twilight Turquoise	253 58920	Twilight Turquoise	723	None	
749	150 (exec. 1271-63F), 210 Series	Tropical Turquoise	253 59787	Tropical Turquoise	757	Argent Silver	2894202
749	Bel Air (exc. 1064DF)	Tropical Turquoise	253 59787	Tropical Turquoise	757	None	
750	150 (exc. 1271) Series	Calypso Cream	253 90209	Calypso Cream	790	Onyx Black	2532247
752	210 Series	Inca Silver	887 56303	Inca Silver	759	Onyx Black	2532247
752	Bel Air Series	Inca Silver	887 56303	Inca Silver	759	None	

1956 TWO TONE COLOR COMBINATIONS

Comb. No.	Model Usage	Upper Body Color	Upper Body Duco No.	Lower Body Color	Lower Body Duco No.	Wheel Color	Dulux No.	Wheel Striping Color	Wheel Striping Duco No
96	150, 210 Series	Crocus Yellow	25358763	Onyx Black	2532247	Crocus Yellow	725	Onyx Black	2532247
96	Bel Air Series	Crocus Yellow	25358763	Onyx Black	2532247	Crocus Yellow	725	None	
00	Bel Air Series	Sierra Gold	28659894	Adobe Beige	25359895	Sierra Gold	742	None	
01	150, 210 Series	India Ivory	25358458	Onyx Black	2532247	Onyx Black	505	Argent Silver	2894202
01	Bel Air Series	India Ivory	25358458	Onyx Black	2532247	Onyx Black	505	None	
02	150, 210 Series	Sherwood Green	28659525	Pinecrest Green	25358897	Pinecrest Green	716	Onyx Black	2532247
02	Bel Air Series	Sherwood Green	28659525	Pinecrest Green	25358897	Pinecrest Green	716	None	
03	1011-19-37-39	Harbor Blue	28158812	Nassau Blue	25358752	Harbor Blue	719	Argent Silver	2894202
03	Bel Air Series (exc. 1062DF)	Harbor Blue	28158812	Nassau Blue	25358752	Harbor Blue	719	None	
05	150, 210 Series	India Ivory	25358458	Pinecrest Green	25358897	Pinecrest Green	716	Onyx Black	2532247
05	Bel Air Series	India Ivory	25358458	Pinecrest Green	25358897	Pinecrest Green	716	None	
06	150, 210 Series	India Ivory	25358458	Sherwood Green	28659525	Sherwood Green	717	Argent Silver	2894202
06	Bel Air Series (exc. 1062DF)	India Ivory	25358458	Sherwood Green	28659525	Sherwood Green	717	None	
07	150, 210 Series	India Ivory	23358458	Nassau Blue	25358752	Nassau Blue	718	Onyx Black	2532247
07	Bel Air Series	India Ivory	25358458	Nassau Blue	25358752	Nassau Blue	718	None	
08	210 Series	India Ivory	25358458	Dusk Plum	28159238	Dusk Plum	728	Argent Silver	2894202
08	Bel Air Series	India Ivory	25358458	Dusk Plum	28159238	Dusk Plum	728	None	
10	210 Series	India Ivory	25358458	Twilight Turq.	25358920	Twilight Turquoise	723	Argent Silver	2894202
10	Bel Air Series	India Ivory	25358458	Twilight Turq.	25358920	Twilight Turquoise	723	None	
11	150, 210 Series	India Ivory	25358458	Matador Red	25359446	Matador Red	738	Onyx Black	2532247
11	1011D-19D-67D	India Ivory	25358458	Matador Red	25359446	Matador Red	738	None	
15	1037D-39D-62DF-64DF	Matador Red	25359446	Dune Beige	25359144	Matador Red	738	None	
17	210 Series	Crocus Yellow	25358763	Laurel Green	28159423	Laurel Green	730	Argent Silver	2894202
17	Bel Air Series	Crocus Yellow	23358763	Laurel Green	28159423	Laurel Green	730	None	
21	210 Series (exc. 1011A)	India Ivory	25358458	Dawn Gray	28159692	Dawn Gray	755	Onyx Black	2532247
21	Bel Air Series	India Ivory	25358458	Dawn Gray	28159692	Dawn Gray	755	None	
54	210 Series	India Ivory	25358458	Tropical Turq.	25359789	Tropical Turquoise	757	Argent Silver	2894202
54	Bel Air Series	India Ivory	25358458	Tropical Turq.	25359789	Tropical Turquoise	757	None	
55	150 Series	Calypso Cream	25390209	Onyx Black	2532247	Calypso Cream	790	Onyx Black	2532247
56	150, 210 Series (exc. 1271)	Grecian Gold	28190317	Calypso Cream	25390209	Grecian Gold	794	Onyx Black	2532247
56	Bel Air Series	Grecian Gold	28190317	Calypso Cream	25390209	Calypso Cream	790	None	
57	210 Series	Inca Silver	88756303	Imperial Ivory	88559931	Imperial Ivory	799	Onyx Black	2532247
57	Bel Air Series	Inca Silver	88756303	Imperial Ivory	88559931	Inca Silver	759	None	
63	1039D-1062DF-1037D	Matador Red	25359446	Adobe Beige	25359895	Matador Red	738	None	

APPENDIX V 1957 MODELS

1957 CHEVROLET

Model Number	Body Style (passengers)	Production	Price*	Weight (lbs)*
One-Fifty				
1502	sedan, 2dr (6)	70,774	$2096	3207
1503	sedan, 4dr (6)	52,266	2148	3232
1512	sedan, 2dr utility (3)	8,300	1985	3159
1529	Handyman wagon, 2dr (6)	14,740	2407	3402
	Total	146,080		
Two-Ten				
2102	sedan, 2dr (6)	162,090	2222	3221
2103	sedan, 4dr (6)	260,401	2275	3266
2124	Delray club coupe (6)	25,644	2262	3216
2154	sport coupe (6)	22,631	2304	3256
2113	sport sedan (6)	16,178	2370	3316
2129	Handyman wagon, 2dr (6)	17,528	2502	3402
2109	Townsman wagon, 4dr (6)	127,803	2556	3457
2119	Beauville wagon, 4dr (9)	21,083	2663	3556
	Total	653,358		
Bel Air				
2402	sedan, 2dr (6)	62,751	2338	3228
2403	sedan, 4dr (6)	254,331	2390	3272
2454	sport coupe (6)	166,426	2399	3274
2413	sport sedan (6)	137,672	2464	3336
2434	convertible (5)	47,562	2611	3405
2429	Nomad wagon, 2dr (6)	6,534	2857	3461
2409	Townsman wagon, 4dr (6)	27,375	2680	3456
	Total	702,651		

*All prices, weights, and model numbers for cars equipped with standard V-8 manual transmission. Six cylinder models about $100 lower.

1957 ENGINE DATA AND POWER TEAMS

Engine	Models	Cu. In. Displ.	Comp. Ratio	Bore	Stroke	Gross H.P.	Net H.P.	Carburetor	Transmission
Blue Flame 140 — 6 cyl.	PASS.	235	8.0	3-9/16"	3-15/16"	140 @ 4200 RPM	125 @ 4000 RPM	Single Barrel	3-Speed Overdrive Powerglide
Turbo-Fire 265-8 cyl.	PASS.	265	8.0	3-3/4"	3"	162 @ 4400 RPM	137 @ 4000 RPM	2-Barrel	3-Speed Overdrive
Turbo-Fire 283-8 cyl.	PASS.	283	8.5	3-7/8"	3"	185 @ 4600 RPM	150 @ 4200 RPM	2-Barrel	Powerglide Turboglide
Super Turbo-Fire 283 — 8 cyl.	PASS.	283	9.5	3-7/8"	3"	220 @ 4800 RPM	190 @ 4600 RPM	4-Barrel	3-Speed Overdrive Automatic Trans.
8 Cylinder	PASS.	283	9.5	3-7/8"	3"	245 @ 5000 RPM	215 @ 4800 RPM	Dual 4-Barrel	3-Speed Close-Ratio Automatic Trans.
8 Cylinder	PASS	283	9.5	3-7/8"	3"	250 @ 5000 RPM	225 @ 4800 RPM	Fuel Injection	3-Speed Close-Ratio Automatic Trans.
8 Cylinder	PASS.	283	9.5	3-7/8"	3"	270 @ 6000 RPM	230 @ 6000 RPM	Dual 4-Barrel	3-Speed Close-Ratio
8 Cylinder	PASS.	283	10.5	3-7/8"	3"	283 @ 6200 RPM	240 @ 5600 RPM	Fuel Injection	3-Speed Close-Ratio

1957 DIMENSIONS

Dimensions (inches): Wheelbase 115; overall length 200; overall height 59.9 (two-door hardtop 58.5, four-door hardtop and convertible 58.4, station wagons 60.1, Nomad 58.8); overall width 73.9; front track 58; rear track 58.8; ground clearance 6.0.

1957 ACCESSORIES

Air conditioning, electric fender antenna, manual fender antenna left and right, Autronic Eye headlamp control, front and rear basket units, seatbelts, wiring junction block, safetylight bracket, power brakes, locking gas cap, Continental wheel carrier, electric clock, compass, full wheel covers, bumper cushion, tissue dispenser, gasoline filter unit, license plate frame (chrome or gold), glareshades, bumper guards, door edge guards, shoulder harness, heater & defroster, horn with third note, tool kit, Kool Kooshion, back-up lamps, courtesy lamps, cigarette lighter, floor mats, outside rearview mirrors, inside non-glare rearview mirror, vanity visor mirror, body sill moulding, lower trunk lid edge moulding, radio (manual, pushbutton, Wonder Bar), armrests, safetylight with mirror, radiator insect screen, electric shaver, door handle shields, parking brake signal, rear seat speaker, wheel spinners, hand portable spotlight, vacuum tank, ventshades, traffic light viewer, outside visors, inside visors, windshield washer (push-button or foot-operated).

1957 TRIM COMBINATION CHART

Comb. No.	Material	Models
650	Black and Gray Cloth	1211-11B-
	Black Imitation Leather	1219
651	Black and Gray Imitation Leather	
	Black Imitation Leather	1271
652	Black and Gray Imitation Leather	
	Black Imitation Leather	1263F
653	Green and Gray Imitation Leather	
	Med. Met. Green Imitation Leather	1263F
654	Charcoal Cloth	1011-19-37-
	Ivory Imitation Leather	39
655	Medium Green Cloth	1011-19-37-
	Light Green Imitation Leather	39
656	Medium Blue Cloth	1011-19-37-
	Light Blue Imitation Leather	39
657	Charcoal Imitation Leather	
	Ivory Imitation Leather	1011A
658	Med. Met. Green Imitation Leather	
	Light Green Imitation Leather	1011A
659	Beige Imitation Leather	

Comb. No.	Material	Models
	Met. Copper Imitation Leather	1011A
660	Charcoal Imitation Leather	1062F-63F-
	Ivory Imitation Leather	62FC
661	Met. Med. Green Imitation Leather	1062F-63F-
	Light Green Imitation Leather	62FC
662	Met. Copper Imitation Leather	1062F-63F-
	Beige Imitation Leather	62FC
663	Black and Silver Cloth	
	Silver Imitation Leather	1011D-19D
664	Black and Green Cloth	
	Med. Met. Green Imitation Leather	1011D-19D
665	Black and Blue Cloth	
	Medium Blue Imitation Leather	1011D-19D
666	Black and Turquoise Cloth	
	Med. Turquoise Imitation Leather	1011D-19D
667	Black and Copper Cloth	
	Beige Imitation Leather	1011D-19D
668	Black and Yellow Cloth	
	Yellow Imitation Leather	1011D-19D
669	Black and Red Cloth	
	Red Imitation Leather	1011D-19D
670	Black and Silver Cloth	
	Silver Imitation Leather	1037D-39D
671	Black & Dark Green Pat. Cloth	
	Med. Met. Green Imitation Leather	1037D-39D

672	Black and Dark Blue Cloth	
	Medium Blue Imitation Leather	1037D-39D
673	Black & Dark Turquoise Cloth	
	Med. Turquoise Imitation Leather	1037D-39D
674	Black and Copper Cloth	
	Beige Imitation Leather	1037D-39D
675	Black and Yellow Cloth	
	Yellow Imitation Leather	1037D-39D
676	Black and Red Cloth	
	Red Imitation Leather	1037D-39D
677	Met. Silver Imitation Leather	
	Ivory Imitation Leather	1067D
678	Med. Met. Green Imitation Leather	
	Light Green Imitation Leather	1067D
679	Medium Blue Imitation Leather	
	Light Blue Imitation Leather	1067D
680	Med. Turquoise Imitation Leather	
	Ivory Imitation Leather	1067D
681	Met. Copper Imitation Leather	
	Beige Imitation Leather	1067D
682	Met. Silver Imitation Leather	
	Yellow Imitation Leather	1067D
683	Met. Silver Imitation Leather	
	Red Imitation Leather	1067D
684	Black and Silver Cloth	
	Silver Met. Imitation Leather	1062DF

685	Black and Dark Green Cloth	
	Med. Met. Green Imitation Leather	1062DF
686	Black and Dark Blue Cloth	
	Medium Blue Imitation Leather	1062DF
687	Black and Dark Turquoise Cloth	
	Med. Turquoise Imitation Leather	1062DF
688	Black and Copper Cloth	
	Beige Imitation Leather	1062DF
689	Black and Yellow Cloth	
	Yellow Imitation Leather	1062DF
690	Black and Red Cloth	
	Red Imitation Leather	1062DF
691	Black and Silver Cloth	
	Silver Imitation Leather	1064DF
692	Black and Dark Green Cloth	
	Medium Green Imitation Leather	1064DF
693	Black and Dark Blue Cloth	
	Medium Blue Imitation Leather	1064DF
694	Black and Dark Turquoise Cloth	
	Medium Turquoise Imitation Leather	1064DF
695	Black and Copper Cloth	
	Beige Imitation Leather	1064DF
696	Black and Yellow Cloth	
	Yellow Imitation Leather	1064DF
697	Black and Red Cloth	
	Red Imitation Leather	1064DF

1957 PAINT COMBINATION CHART

Comb. No.	Model Usage	Body		Wheel Color	
		Color	*Duco. No.*	*Color*	*Dulux No.*
793	150, 210, Bel Air	Onyx Black	253-2247	Black	505
794	150 (ex. 1529), 210, Bel Air (ex. 2409-29)	Imperial Ivory	885-59931	Imperial Ivory	799
795	150, 210, Bel Air	Larkspur Blue	253-90114	Larkspur Blue	808
796	150, 210, Bel Air	Harbor Blue	281-58812	Harbor Blue	719
797	150, 210, Bel Air	Surf Green	253-90147	Surf Green	807
798	150, 210, Bel Air	Highland Green	286-59775	Highland Green	822
799	150 (exc. 1508), 210, Bel Air	Tropical Turquoise	253-59787	Tropical Turquoise	757
800	150 (exc. 1508), 210, Bel Air	Colonial Cream	253-58094	Colonial Cream	809
801	Bel Air Conv.	Canyon Coral	253-90645	Canyon Coral	821
802	150, 210, Bel Air	Matador Red	253-59446	Matador Red	738
803	Bel Air Conv.	Coronado Yellow	253-90620	Coronado Yellow	819
804	210, Bel Air	Inca Silver	887-56303	Inca Silver	759
805	2124-09-19-29, Bel Air	Sierra Gold	286-59894	Sierra Gold	742
806	150 (exc. 1508), 210, Bel Air	Adobe Beige	253-59895	Adobe Beige	760
821	Bel Air Conv.	Dusk Pearl	887-90354	Dusk Pearl	812
823	Bel Air Conv.	Laurel Green	281-90596	Laurel Green	806

1957 TWO TONE COLOR COMBINATIONS

Comb. No.	Model Usage	Upper Body		Lower Body		Wheel Color	
		Color	Duco No.	Color	Duco No.	Color	Dulux No.
807	150 (exc. 1508), 210, Bel Air (exc. Conv.)	India Ivory	253-58458	Onyx Black	253-2247	Black	505
808	150 (exc. 1508), 210, Bel Air (exc. Conv.)	Imperial Ivory	885-59931	Inca Silver	887-56303	Inca Silver	759
809	150 (exc. 1508), Bel Air (exc. Conv.) 210	— Harbor Blue	— 281-58812	Harbor Blue Larkspur Blue	281-58812 253-90114	Harbor Blue Larkspur Blue	719 808
810	150 (ex. 1508), 210, Bel Air (exc. Conv.)	India Ivory	253-58458	Larkspur Blue	253-90114	Larkspur Blue	808
811	150 (ex. 1508), 210, Bel Air (exc. Conv.)	India Ivory	253-58458	Tropical Turquoise	253-59787	Tropical Turquoise	757
812	150 (exc. 1508) 210 Bel Air (exc. Conv.)	— Surf Green Surf Green	— 253-90147 253-90147	Surf Green Highland Green Highland Green	253-90147 286-59775 286-59775	Surf Green Surf Green Highland Green	807 807 822
813	150 (exc. 1508), 210, Bel Air (exc. Conv.)	India Ivory	253-58458	Surf Green	253-90147	Surf Green	807
814	210, Bel Air (exc. Conv.)	India Ivory	253-58458	Coronado Yellow	253-90620	Coronado Yellow	819
815	150 (exc. 1508), Bel Air (exc. Conv. 210	— Colonial Cream	— 253-58094	Colonial Cream Onyx Black	253-58094 253-2247	Colonial Cream Black	809 505
816	150 (exc. 1508), Bel Air (exc. Conv.) 210	— Colonial Cream	— 253-58094	Colonial Cream India Ivory	253-58094 253-58458	Colonial Cream Colonial Cream	809 809
817	210, Bel Air (exc. Conv.)	India Ivory	253-58458	Canyon Coral	253-90645	Canyon Coral	821
818	2124-09-19-29 Bel Air (exc. Conv.)	Adobe Beige	253-59895	Sierra Gold	286-59894	Sierra Gold	742
819	150 (exc. 1508), 210, Bel Air (exc. Conv.)	India Ivory	253-58458	Matador Red	253-59446	Matador Red	738
820	210 Bel Air (exc. Conv.)	Colonial Cream —	253-58094 —	Laurel Green Laurel Green	281-90596 281-90596	Colonial Cream Laurel Green	809 806
822	210 Bel Air (Exc. Conv.)	Dusk Pearl —	887-90354 —	Imperial Ivory Dusk Pearl	885-59931 887-90354	Dusk Pearl Dusk Pearl	812 812

Glossary

"A" pillar: The front post supporting an automobile top where it joins the windshield.*

"B" pillar: The central or middle post (lacking in hardtop models).*

"C" pillar: The rear post of an automobile top (except on station wagons, which have a "D" pillar).*

"D" pillar: The fourth post supporting an automobile top found only in station wagons and some special-order bodies.*

Backlight: Rear window glass.

Beltline: Horizontal line on an automobile which separates the glass area from the body.

Cowl panel: The sheet metal from the base of the windshield forward to the cut-line of the hood, between the front fenders.*

Greenhouse: Side glass area between the body and the roof.

Green-sand casting: A green-sand core was used to eliminate the dry sand core so that the block could be turned upside down, cast upside down so the plate that holds the bore cores could be accurately located. This way it could be cast down to 5/32nds jacket walls.**

Pounds-feet: This physics term measuring torque was evoked by scientists. "Foot pound," used in some magazines is incorrect, though it might sound better.

Seating buck: A mock-up of the car's interior, from which dimensions and space requirements can be figured: for headroom, leg room, hip room, etc.

Template: A metal or wood profile pattern of a surface or section.*

Track: Space between left and right wheels at front and rear. "Tread," as used in some magazines is incorrect.

Tumblehome: The slant or angle-from-vertical, in the side window area or "greenhouse" of an automobile.

* From "The Look of Cars" by Henry B. Lent. Pgs. 152-153.
** From *Special Interest Autos*, Number 27, p. 17.

Index

ILLUSTRATIONS

NOTE: Numbers in italics refer to illustrations in color, pages 97-104